THE DIVINE LITURGY

A HYMNAL IN GREEK AND ENGLISH

The Divine Liturgy—A Hymnal in Greek and English
Musical selections © 1997 by Kevin Lawrence.
All rights reserved.

ISBN 0-9650957-2-X

Permission to use
The Divine Liturgy of St. John Chrysostom
translated by the faculty of Holy Cross Greek
Orthodox School of Theology (Brookline, MA,
Holy Cross Orthodox Press, 1985) is gratefully
acknowledged.

Additional copies of this volume are available from
Kevin Lawrence, choir director,
Dormition of the Theotokos Greek Orthodox Church
800 Westridge Road
Greensboro, NC 27410
336 784-5128

or from

Assumption Greek Orthodox Church Bookstore
8202 East Cactus Road
Scottsdale, AZ 85260
480 991-3009

CONTENTS

Introduction vii
A note on the transliteration   viii

THE GREAT DOXOLOGY 2/3

THE DIVINE LITURGY 18/19

VARIABLE HYMNS FOR THE DIVINE LITURGY

Apolitikia
     Sunday Resurrectional Apolitikia
Tone 1   .   .   .   .   .   . 98/99
Tone 2   .   .   .   .   .   . 102/103
Tone 3   .   .   .   .   .   . 106/107
Tone 4   .   .   .   .   .   . 110/111
Tone 5   .   .   .   .   .   . 114/115
Tone 6   .   .   .   .   .   . 118/119
Tone 7   .   .   .   .   .   . 122/123
Tone 8   .   .   .   .   .   . 126/127

     Apolitikia from the Triodion
First Sunday of Lent—Sunday of Orthodoxy   . 128/129
Second Sunday of Lent—St. Gregory Palamas   . 132/133
Third Sunday of Lent—as on September 14   . 180/181
Fourth Sunday of Lent—St. John of *The Ladder*   . 136/137

Fifth Sunday of Lent—St. Mary of Egypt   . 140/141
Lazarus Saturday and Palm Sunday   .   . 144/145
Palm Sunday—another apolitikion   .   . 148/149

     Apolitikia from the Pentecostarion
Pascha 152/153
Sunday of Thomas 154/155

Sunday of the Myrrh-bearing Women . . 158/159
Sunday of the Myrrh-bearing Women: another
  apolitikion 162/163
Mid-Pentecost/Sunday of the Samaritan Woman 166/167
The Ascension of the Lord . . . 168/169
Sunday of the Holy Fathers . . . 170/171
Pentecost 172/173
Sunday of All Saints 174/175

Apolitikia from the Menaion
September 8—The Birth of the Theotokos . 176/177
September 14—The Elevation of the Holy Cross 180/181
November 21—The Entry of the Theotokos into
  the Temple 182/183
Sunday of the Holy Ancestors of Christ . 186/187
Preparation of the Nativity of the Lord . 190/191
Sunday before the Nativity of the Lord . 194/195
December 25—The Nativity of the Lord . 198/199
Sunday after the Nativity of the Lord . . 202/203
Preparation of Theophany . . . 204/205
January 6—Theophany 209/210
February 2—The Presentation of the Lord in the
  Temple 212/213
March 25—Annunciation 216/217
August 6—The Transfiguration of the Lord . 220/221
August 15—The Dormition of the Theotokos 222/223

Kontakia
Ordinary Kontakion 224/225
September 8—The Birth of the Theotokos . 228/229
September 14—The Exaltation of the Holy Cross 232/233
November 21—The Entry of the Theotokos into
  the Temple 236/237
The Season before the Nativity of the Lord . 240/241
December 25—The Nativity of the Lord . 244/245

January 6—Theophany 248/249
February 2—The Presentation of the Lord in the
    Temple 250/251
Sunday of the Publican and the Pharisee . 254/255
Sunday of the Prodigal Son . . . 256/257
Sunday of the Last Judgement . . . 260/261
Sunday of Forgiveness 264/265
March 25—Annunciation . . . 268/269
Palm Sunday 272/273
Pascha 274/275
The Ascension of the Lord . . . 278/279
Pentecost 280/281
Sunday of All Saints 282/283
August 6—The Transfiguration of the Lord . 284/285
August 15—The Dormition of the Theotokos 288/289

Hymns sung instead of the Trisagion
September 14 and The Third Sunday of Lent
    (Ton stavron su) 290/291
Pascha, Pentecost, Nativity of the Lord, Baptisms
    (Osi is Hriston) 292/293

Alternate Cherubic Hymn . . . 294/295

Megalynaria
At the Liturgy of St. Basil 298/299
Palm Sunday 302/303
Pascha 304/305
Sunday of Thomas 308/309
Pentecost 310/311
The Nativity of the Lord 312/313

Communion Hymns

Saturday of Lazarus	316
Palm Sunday	317
Pascha	318
Sunday of Thomas	320
The Ascension of the Lord	321
Pentecost	322
Sunday of All Saints	323
September 8—The Birth of the Theotokos	324
September 14—The Exaltation of the Holy Cross	325
December 25—The Nativity of the Lord	326
January 6—Theophany	327
January 7—St. John the Forerunner and Baptist	328
March 25—The Annunciation	329
August 6—The Transfiguration of the Lord	330

HYMNS FOR OTHER DIVINE SERVICES

Vespers

Kirie ekekraxa/O Lord I call upon You	332/333
Fos ilaron/Radiant light	336/337
O Kirios evasilefsen/The Lord is King	340
Tis Theos/Who is so great a God	341
Plusii eptohefsan/Many who are wealthy	342

Hierarchical Services

Ton Thespotin	343

Salutations

Here Nimfi/Rejoice, O Bride	344/345
Tin oreotita/When he beheld the beauty	344/345

Pascha: Before the service at midnight

Thevte lavete fos/Come receive the light	348/349
Tin anastasin/Heaven's angels	348/349

Wedding Service

Isaia horeve/O Isaiah 350/351

Agii martires/O holy martyrs   .   .   .   352/353

Thoxa si Hriste/Glory to You, O Christ .   .   352/353

Services for the Departed

Meta ton Agion/Among the saints   .   .   354/355

Eonia i mnimi/Memory eternal   356

PRAYERS

Preparation for Holy Communion   .   .   .   358

Thanksgiving after Holy Communion   .   .   360

Stewardship Prayer   362

INDEX OF GREEK TITLES   363

Introduction

The liturgical services of the Orthodox Church developed before the invention of printing, yet presuppose the active participation of the faithful. In earlier centuries, the services became familiar to the assembly by a process of rote learning. In our age of the printed word and of universal literacy, a book such as this one can permit a greater degree of congregational participation than may have been easily possible in ages past. The ultimate goal remains a degree of familiarity with the services such that a congregational service book will hardly be needed. The words and melodies of the services thus take root in our hearts, coming to mind throughout our days and bearing fruit in every aspect of our lives.

As congregations of the Greek Orthodox Archdiocese adjust to using English as a liturgical language, a necessary sense of continuity can be provided by keeping musical settings of English texts closely related to the neo-Byzantine melodies best known to Greek Orthodox Americans. Some adjustments to received melodies must certainly be made if music and text are to fit together in a natural and convincing way, with the music serving the message of the English text. In this volume, most changes to received melodies have been made in accordance with the musical grammar of neo-Byzantine chant; lowest priority has been given to conventions regarding number of notes per syllable. Though the resulting compositions are admittedly derivative, I believe that this approach better serves the objective of popular participation than would a newly composed repertoire of melodies.

For the non-musical elements of the Divine Liturgy, this book uses the English translation by the faculty of Holy Cross Greek Orthodox School of Theology, with the kind permission of Holy Cross Press. Musical settings from page 19 to page 95 use an English translation developed by a committee appointed by the Standing Conference of the Canonical Orthodox Bishops in America. Translations of other hymns are based on the work of the Monks of New Skete. Every attempt has been made to insure consistency of style and vocabulary, in spite of the differing sources of the English texts.

This book is an outgrowth of a hymnal project for the 1996 Archdiocesan Clergy Laity Congress, undertaken under the sponsorship of the National Forum of Greek Orthodox Church Musicians. I am grateful to Vicki Pappas, George Raptis, Peter Vatsures, Nicolas

Maragos and Toula Chininis of the National Forum, for their valuable advice during the first phase of the development of this hymnal. I wish to extend my thanks also to Father Nicholas Triantafilou of Holy Trinity Cathedral, Charlotte, North Carolina, to Father Stelyios Muksuris, also of Holy Trinity, and to Joanna Cavalaris, Holy Trinity's choir director, for their assistance and encouragement during the preparation of the hymnal's final version.

Kevin Lawrence
August 6, 1997
The Transfiguration of the Lord

A note on the transliteration

For the convenience of those whose reading knowledge of Greek is minimal, this hymnal includes a phonetic transliteration of all Greek hymns. The transliteration follows the system used in works published by the Department of Religious Education of the Greek Orthodox Archdiocese. While careful listening to fluent Greek speakers will be the best guide to pronunciation, the following explanation may be helpful. In the system of phonetics used in this book:

a is pronounced as in the English word f*a*ther
e is pronounced as in the English word m*e*t
i is pronounced as in the English word s*ee*
o is pronounced as in the English word h*o*pe
u is pronounced as in the English word t*oo*
x is pronounced as in the English word bo*x*
z is pronounced as in the English word *z*ip
ng (Greek γγ) is pronounced as in the English word si*ng*

Informal transliteration systems such as this one transcribe the Greek letter γ variously as *g, y* or *gh*. The letter *g* (as in the English word *g*ood), is used consistently throughout this book.

The Greek letters Δ, δ and Θ, θ are both transliterated here as *th*. The former is voiced (as in *th*is), the latter voiceless (as in *th*ick). Reference to the original Greek letter, or attentive listening, is needed to differentiate the two sounds.

Other consonants are pronounced as in English.

THE GREAT DOXOLOGY AND DIVINE LITURGY

Great Doxology   2
Resurrectional Troparion   .   .   .   16
Divine Liturgy   18

Πρίν τῆς ἐνάρξεως τῆς Θείας Λειτουργίας,
ψάλλεται ἡ κατακλείδα τοῦ Ὄρθρου·

Η ΜΕΓΑΛΗ ΔΟΞΟΛΟΓΙΑ

Δό - ξα σοι τῷ δεί - ξαν - τι τὸ φῶς.
Tho - xa si to thi - xan - di to fos.

Δό - ξα ἐν ὑ - ψί - στοις Θε - ῷ καὶ ε - πὶ γῆς εἰ -
Tho-xa en i - psi - stis The - o ke e - pi gis i -

ρή - νη ἐν ἀν - θρώ - ποις εὐ - δο - κί - α.
ri - ni en an - thro - pis ev-tho - ki - a.

Ὑ - μνοῦ - μέν σε, εὐ - λο - γοῦ-μέν σε, προσ-κυ -
I - mnu - men se, ev - lo - gu-men se, pros-ki -

νοῦ-μέν σε, δο - ξο - λο - γοῦ-μέν σε, εὐ-χα - ρι -
nu-men se, tho - xo - lo - gu-men se, ev-ha - ri -

στοῦ-μέν σοι δι-ὰ τὴν με-γά-λην σου δό - ξαν.
stu-men si thi-a tin me-ga-lin su tho - xan.

2

THE GREAT DOXOLOGY

1. Glo-ry to You, O Giv-er of light. Glo-ry to God in the high-est and on earth peace, good will a-mong all peo - ple.

2. We praise You, we bless You, we wor-ship You, we glo-ri-fy You, we give thanks to You for Your great glo - ry.

3

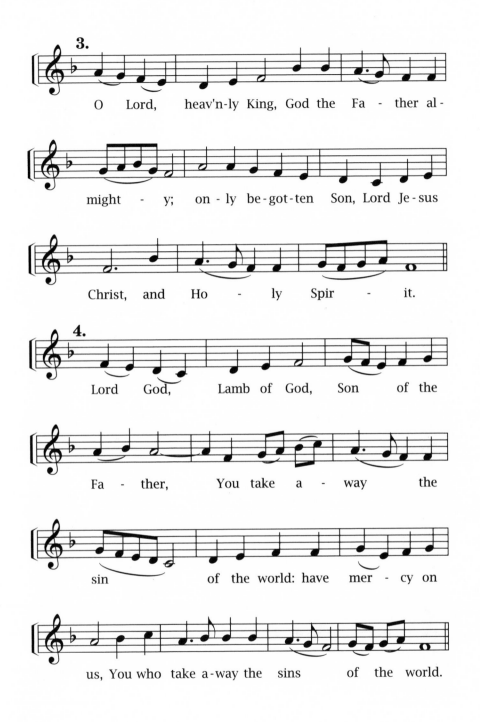

3. O Lord, heav'n-ly King, God the Fa - ther al - might - y; on - ly be - got - ten Son, Lord Je - sus Christ, and Ho - ly Spir - it.

4. Lord God, Lamb of God, Son of the Fa - ther, You take a - way the sin of the world: have mer - cy on us, You who take a - way the sins of the world.

5

5.

Πρόσ - δε - ξαι τὴν δέ - η - σιν ἡ - μῶν ὁ κα -
Pros - the - xe tin the - i - sin i - mon o ka -

θή - με - νος ἐν δε - ξι - ᾷ τοῦ Πα - τρὸς καὶ ἐ -
thi - me - nos en the - xi - a tu Pa - tros ke e -

λέ - η - σον ἡ - μᾶς.
le - i - son i - mas.

6.

Ὅ - τι σὺ εἶ μό - νος Ἅ - γι - ος
O - ti si i mo - nos A - yi - os

σὺ εἶ μό - νος Κύ - ρι - ος Ἰ - η - σοῦς Χρι -
si - i mo - nos Ki - ri - os I - i - sus Hri -

στὸς εἰς δό - ξαν Θε - οῦ Πα - τρὸς. Ἀ - μήν.
stos is tho - xan The - u Pa - tros. A - min.

7.

Κα' - θέ - κά - στην ἡ - μέ - ραν εὐ - λο - γή - σω σε καὶ αἰ -
Ka - the - ka - stin i - me - ran ev - lo - yi - so se ke e -

6

5. Re - ceive our prayer, You who

sit at the Fa - ther's right, and have mer - cy on us.

6. For on - ly You are the Ho - ly One,

on - ly You are the Lord, Je - sus Christ, to the

glo - ry of God the Fa - ther. A - men.

7. Ev - 'ry day will I bless you; I will

νέ - σω τὸ ὄ - νο - μά σου εἰς τὸν αἰ - ῶ - να
ne - so to o - no - ma su is ton e - o - na

καὶ εἰς τὸν αἰ - ῶ - να τοῦ αἰ - ῶ - νος.
ke is ton e - o - na tu e - o - nos.

8.

Κα - τα - ξί - ω - σον Κύ - ρι - ε ἐν τῇ ἡ - μέ - ρᾳ ταύ -
Ka - ta - xi - o - son Ki - ri - e en ti i - me - ra taf -

τη ἀ - να - μαρ - τή - τους φυ - λαχ - θῆ - ναι ἡ - μᾶς.
ti a - na - mar - ti - tus fi - lah - thi - ne i - mas.

9.

Εὐ - λο - γη - τὸς εἶ Κί - ρι - ε ὁ Θε - ὸς τῶν πα - τέ -
Ev - lo - gi - tos i Ki - ri - e o The - os ton pa - te -

ρων ἡ - μῶν καὶ αἰ - νε - τὸν καὶ δε - δο - ξα - σμέ - νον τὸ
ron i - mon ke e - ne - ton ke the - tho - xa - sme - non to

ὄ - νο - μά σου εἰς τοὺς αἰ - ῶ - νας. Ἀ - μήν.
o - no - ma su is tus e - o - nas. A - min.

praise Your name for-ev - er, to the

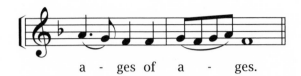

a - ges of a - ges.

8. Count us wor - thy, Lord, of pass - ing this

day with - out sin.

9. Bless - ed are You, O Lord, God of our

fa - thers; Your name is praised and

glo - ri fied for - ev - er. A - men.

9

10

Let Your mer - cy de - scend up - on

us, O Lord, for we place our hope in You.

11.

Bless - ed are You, O Lord, bless - ed are You;

teach me Your com - mand - ments.(3)

12.

You have been our ref - uge, Lord, from one gen - e -

ra - tion to the next. I cried out:

Lord, have mer - cy on me.

ἴ - α-σαι τὴν ψυ - χήν μου ὅ-τι ἥ-μαρ-τόν σοι.
i - a-se tin psi - hin mu o-ti i-mar-ton si.

13.

Κύ-ρι-ε πρὸς σὲ κα-τέ-φυ-γον δι-δα-ξόν με
Ki-ri-e pros se ka-te-fi-gon thi-tha-xon me

τοῦ ποι-εῖν τὸ θέ-λη-μά σου, ὅ-τι σὺ εἶ ὁ Θε-ός μου.
tu pi-in to the-li-ma su, o-ti si i o The-os mu.

14.

Ὅ - τι πα-ρὰ σοι πη-γὴ ζω-ῆς ἐν τῷ φω-
O - ti pa-ra si pi-gi zo-is en to fo-

τί σου ὀ - ψό - με-θα φῶς.
ti su o - pso - me-tha fos.

15.

Πα-ρά-τει - νον τὸ ἔ-λε-ός σου
Pa-ra-ti - non to e-le-os su

τοῖς γι - νώ - σκου - σί σε.
tis gi - no - sku - si se.

12

Heal my soul, for I have sinned a-gainst You.

13. I run to You, O Lord; teach me to please You, for You are my God.

14. For in You is the foun - tain of life, and in Your light we see light.

15. Pour forth Your mer - cy on those who know You.

"Α - γι - ος ὁ Θε - ὸς, ἅ - γι - ος Ἰ-σχυ-ρὸς,
A - gi-os o The-os, a - gi-os Is-hi-ros,

ἅ - γι - ος Ἀ - θά - να-τος, ἐ - λέ - η-σον ἡ - μᾶς.(3)
a - gi-os A - tha-na-tos, e - le - i-son i - mas.(3)

Δό - ξα Πα-τρὶ καὶ Υἱ - ῷ καὶ Ἁ-γί - ῳ Πνεύ-μα-τι· καὶ
Tho-xa Pa-tri ke I - o ke A-gi-o Pnev-ma-ti; ke

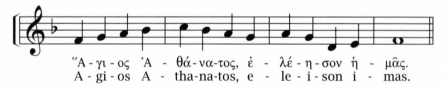

νῦν καὶ ἀ - εὶ καὶ εἰς τοὺς αἰ-ῶ-νας τῶν αἰ - ώ-νων. Ἀ - μήν.
nin ke a - i ke is tus e-o-nas ton e - o-non. A - min.

"Α - γι - ος Ἀ - θά - να-τος, ἐ - λέ - η-σον ἡ - μᾶς.
A - gi-os A - tha-na-tos, e - le - i-son i - mas.

"Α - γι - ος ὁ Θε - ὸς, ἅ - γι - ος Ἰ-σχυ - ρὸς,
A - gi-os o The - os, a - gi-os Is - hi - ros,

ἅ - γι - ος Ἀ - θά - να-τος, ἐ - λέ - η-σον ἡ - μᾶς.
a - gi-os A - tha-na-tos, e - le - i-son i - mas.

14

Ho - ly God, ho - ly Might - y,

ho - ly Im - mor - tal, have mer - cy on us.(3)

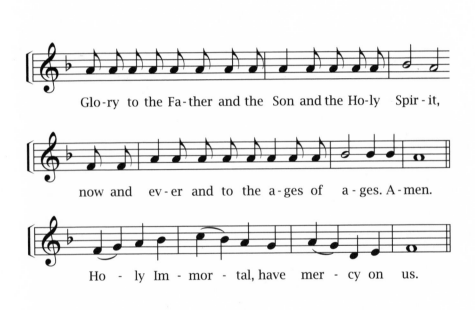

Glo-ry to the Fa-ther and the Son and the Ho-ly Spir-it,

now and ev-er and to the a-ges of a-ges. A-men.

Ho - ly Im - mor - tal, have mer - cy on us.

Ho - ly God, ho - ly Might - y,

ho - ly Im - mor - tal, have mer - cy on us.

Σή - με - ρον σω - τη - ρί - α τῷ κό - σμῳ
Si - me - ron so - ti - ri - a to ko - smo

γέ - γο - νεν. Ἄ - σω - μεν τῷ ἀ - να -
ye - yo - nen. A - so - men to a - na -

στάν - τι ἐκ τά - φου καὶ ἀρ - χη -
stan - di ek ta - fu ke ar - hi -

γῷ τῆς ζω - ῆς ἡ - μῶν· Κα - θε -
yo tis zo - is i - mon; Ka - the -

λὼν γὰρ τῷ θα - νά - τῳ τὸν θά - να - τον, τὸ
lon yar to tha - na - to ton tha - na - ton, to

νῖ - κος ἔ - δω - κεν ἡ - μῖν καὶ τὸ μέ - γα
ni - kos e - tho - ken i - min ke to me - ya

ἔ - λε - ος.
e - le - os.

On feast days we sing the apolitikion of the feast after the Great Doxology. On ordinary Sundays we sing the following resurrectional troparion:

To - day sal-va - tion has come to all the world. Let us sing to Him who rose from the grave, the ver - y source of our life. By His own death He de - stroyed death, be - stow-ing on us vic-to-ry and His great mer - cy.

Η ΘΕΙΑ ΛΕΙΤΟΥΡΓΙΑ

Ἱερεύς· Εὐλογημένη ἡ βασιλεία τοῦ Πατρὸς καὶ τοῦ Υἱοῦ καὶ τοῦ Ἁγίου Πνεύματος, νῦν καὶ ἀεὶ καὶ εἰς τοὺς αἰῶνας τῶν αἰώνων.
Λαός·

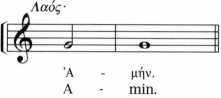

'Α - μήν.
A - min.

Η ΜΕΓΑΛΗ ΣΥΝΑΠΤΗ

Ἱερεύς· Ἐν εἰρήνῃ τοῦ Κυρίου δεηθῶμεν.
Λαός·

Κύ - ρι - ε, 'λέ - η - σον.
Ki - ri - e, 'le - i - son.

Ἱερεύς· Ὑπὲρ τῆς ἄνωθεν εἰρήνης καὶ τῆς σωτηρίας τῶν ψυχῶν ἡμῶν, τοῦ Κυρίου δεηθῶμεν.
Λαός·

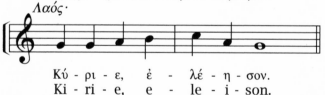

Κύ - ρι - ε, ἐ - λέ - η - σον.
Ki - ri - e, e - le - i - son.

Ἱερεύς· Ὑπὲρ τῆς εἰρήνης τοῦ σύμπαντος κόσμου, εὐσταθείας τῶν ἁγίων τοῦ Θεοῦ Ἐκκλησιῶν καὶ τῆς τῶν πάντων ἑνώσεως, τοῦ Κυρίου δεηθῶμεν.
Λαός·

Κύ - ρι - ε, ἐ - λέ - η - σον.
Ki - ri - e, e - le - i - son.

THE DIVINE LITURGY

Priest: Blessed is the kingdom of the
+ Father and the Son and the Holy Spirit,
now and ever and to the ages of ages.
People:

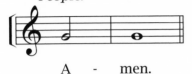

A - men.

*During the Paschal season we
sing Χριστὸς ἀνέστη / Christ is risen
3 times. See pages 152/153.*

THE GREAT LITANY

Priest: In peace let us pray to the Lord.
People:

Lord, have mer - cy.

Priest: For the peace of God and the salvation
of our souls, let us pray to the Lord.
People:

Lord, have mer - cy.

Priest: For peace in the whole world, for the
stability of the holy churches of God, and
the unity of all, let us pray to the Lord.
People:

Lord, have mer - cy.

19

Ἱερεύς· Ὑπὲρ τοῦ ἁγίου οἴκου τούτου καὶ τῶν μετὰ πίστεως, εὐλαβείας καὶ φόβου Θεοῦ εἰσιόντων ἐν αὐτῷ, τοῦ Κυρίου δεηθῶμεν.
Λαός·

Κύ - ρι - ε, 'λέ - η - σον.
Ki - ri - e, 'le - i - son.

Ἱερεύς· Ὑπὲρ τοῦ Ἀρχιεπισκόπου ἡμῶν *(ὄνομα), καὶ τοῦ* Ἐπισκόπου ἡμῶν *(ὄνομα),* τοῦ τιμίου πρεσβυτερίου, τῆς ἐν Χριστῷ διακονίας, παντὸς τοῦ κλήρου καὶ τοῦ λαοῦ, τοῦ Κυρίου δεηθῶμεν.
Λαός·

Κύ - ρι - ε, ἐ - λέ - η - σον.
Ki - ri - e, e - le - i - son.

Ἱερεύς· Ὑπὲρ τοῦ εὐσεβοῦς ἡμῶν ἔθνους, πάσης ἀρχῆς καὶ ἐξουσίας ἐν αὐτῷ, τοῦ Κυρίου δεηθῶμεν.
Λαός·

Κύ - ρι - ε, ἐ - λέ - η - σον.
Ki - ri - e, e - le - i - son.

Ἱερεύς· Ὑπὲρ τῆς κοινότητος καὶ τῆς πόλεως ταύτης, πάσης πόλεως καὶ χώρας καὶ τῶν πίστει οἰκούντων ἐν αὐταῖς, τοῦ Κυρίου δεηθῶμεν.
Λαός·

Κύ - ρι - ε, 'λέ - η - σον.
Ki - ri - e, 'le - i - son.

Ἱερεύς· Ὑπὲρ εὐκρασίας ἀέρων, εὐφορίας τῶν καρπῶν τῆς γῆς καὶ καιρῶν εἰρηνικῶν, τοῦ Κυρίου δεηθῶμεν.
Λαός·

Κύ - ρι - ε, ἐ - λέ - η - σον.
Ki - ri - e, e - le - i - son.

Priest: For this holy house and for those who enter it with faith, reverence and the fear of God, let us pray to the Lord.
People:

Lord, have mer - cy.

Priest: For our Archbishop *[name]*, our Bishop *[name]*, the honorable presbyters, for the deacons in the service of Christ, and all the clergy and laity, let us pray to the Lord.
People:

Lord, have mer - cy.

Priest: For our country, the president, and all those in public service, let us pray to the Lord.
People:

Lord, have mer - cy.

Priest: For this parish and city, for every city and country, and for the faithful who live in them, let us pray to the Lord.
People:

Lord, have mer - cy.

Priest: For favorable weather, an abundance of the fruits of the earth, and temperate seasons, let us pray to the Lord.
People:

Lord, have mer - cy.

Ἱερεύς· Ὑπὲρ πλεόντων, ὁδοιπορούντων, ἀεροπορούντων, νοσούντων, καμνόντων, αἰχμαλώτων καὶ τῆς σωτηρίας αὐτῶν, τοῦ Κυρίου δεηθῶμεν.

Λαός·

Κύ - ρι - ε, ἐ - λέ - η - σον.
Ki - ri - e, e - le - i - son.

Ἱερεύς· Ὑπὲρ τοῦ ῥυσθῆναι ἡμᾶς ἀπὸ πάσης θλίψεως, ὀργῆς, κινδύνου καὶ ἀνάγκης, τοῦ Κυρίου δεηθῶμεν.

Λαός·

Κύ - ρι - ε, ᾽λέ - η - σον.
Ki - ri - e, ᾽le - i - son.

Ἱερεύς· Ἀντιλαβοῦ, σῶσον, ἐλέησον καὶ διαφύλαξον ἡμᾶς, ὁ Θεός, τῇ σῇ χάριτι.

Λαός·

Κύ - ρι - ε, ἐ - λέ - η - σον.
Ki - ri - e, e - le - i - son.

Ἱερεύς· Τῆς παναγίας, ἀχράντου, ὑπερευλογημένης, ἐνδόξου δεσποίνης ἡμῶν Θεοτόκου καὶ ἀειπαρθένου Μαρίας, μετὰ πάντων τῶν ἁγίων μνημονεύσαντες, ἑαυτοὺς καὶ ἀλλήλους καὶ πᾶσαν τὴν ζωὴν ἡμῶν Χριστῷ τῷ Θεῷ παραθώμεθα.

Λαός·

Σοί, Κύ - ρι - ε.
Si, Ki - ri - e.

Priest: For travelers by land, sea and air, for the sick, the suffering, the captives, and for their salvation, let us pray to the Lord.
People:

Lord, have mer - cy.

Priest: For our deliverance from all affliction, wrath, danger and distress, let us pray to the Lord.
People:

Lord, have mer - cy.

Priest: Help us, save us, have mercy upon us and protect us, O God, by Your grace.
People:

Lord, have mer - cy.

Priest: Remembering + our most holy, pure, blessed, and glorious Lady, the Theotokos and ever virgin Mary, with all the saints, let us commit ourselves, and one another, and our whole life to Christ our God.
People:

To You, O Lord.

23

Ἱερεύς (χαμηλοφώνως): Κύριε ὁ Θεὸς ἡμῶν, οὗ τὸ κράτος ἀνείκαστον καὶ ἡ δόξα ἀκατάληπτος· οὗ τὸ ἔλεος ἀμέτρητον καὶ ἡ φιλανθρωπία ἄφατος· αὐτὸς Δέσποτα, κατὰ τὴν εὐσπλαγχνίαν σου, ἐπίβλεψον ἐφ᾿ ἡμᾶς καὶ ἐπὶ τὸν ἅγιον οἶκον τοῦτον καὶ ποίησον μεθ᾿ ἡμῶν καὶ τῶν συνευχομένων ἡμῖν πλούσια τὰ ἐλέη σου καὶ τοὺς οἰκτιρμούς σου.

Ἱερεύς·

Ὅτι πρέπει σοι πᾶσα δόξα, τιμὴ καὶ προσκύνησις,
τῷ Πατρὶ καὶ τῷ Υἱῷ καὶ τῷ Ἁγίῳ Πνεύματι,
νῦν καὶ ἀεὶ καὶ εἰς τοὺς αἰῶνας τῶν αἰώνων.
Λαός·

Ἀ - μήν.
A - min.

ΤΟ ΠΡΩΤΟΝ ΑΝΤΙΦΩΝΟΝ

Καὶ ψάλλεται τὸ ἀντίφωνον, συνοδευόμενον ἀπὸ τὸ ἐφύμνιον.
Λαός·

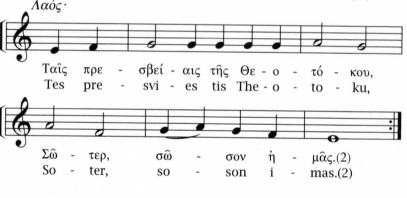

Ταῖς πρε - σβεί - αις τῆς Θε - ο - τό - κου,
Tes pre - svi - es tis The - o - to - ku,

Σῶ - τερ, σῶ - σον ἡ - μᾶς.(2)
So - ter, so - son i - mas.(2)

Ταῖς πρε - σβεί - αις τῆς Θε - ο - τό - κου,
Tes pre - svi - es tis The - o - to - ku,

Σῶ - τερ, σῶ - σον ἡ - μᾶς.
So - ter, so - son i - mas.

24

> *Priest (in a low voice):* Lord our God, whose power is beyond compare and glory beyond understanding; whose mercy is boundless and love for us is ineffable: look on us and upon this holy house in Your compassion. Grant to us and to those who pray with us Your abundant mercy.

Priest: For to You belong all glory, honor and worship, to the + Father and the Son and the Holy Spirit, now and ever and to the ages of ages.
People:

A - men.

THE FIRST ANTIPHON

The designated psalm verses are sung with the refrain.
People:

Through the in - ter - ces-sions of the The - o -

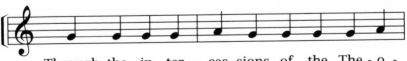

to - kos, Sav - ior, save us.(2)

Through the in - ter - ces-sions of the The - o -

to - kos, Sav - ior, save us.

25

Η ΜΙΚΡΑ ΣΥΝΑΠΤΗ

Ἱερεύς· Ἔτι καὶ ἔτι ἐν εἰρήνῃ τοῦ Κυρίου δεηθῶμεν.
Λαός·

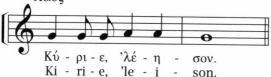

Κύ - ρι - ε, 'λέ - η - σον.
Ki - ri - e, 'le - i - son.

Ἱερεύς· Ἀντιλαβοῦ, σῶσον, ἐλέησον καὶ
διαφύλαξον ἡμᾶς, ὁ Θεός, τῇ σῇ χάριτι.
Λαός·

Κύ - ρι - ε, ἐ - λέ - η - σον.
Ki - ri - e, e - le - i - son.

Ἱερεύς· Τῆς παναγίας, ἀχράντου, ὑπερευλογημένης, ἐνδόξου,
δεσποίνης ἡμῶν Θεοτόκου καὶ ἀειπαρθένου Μαρίας, μετὰ
πάντων τῶν ἁγίων μνημονεύσαντες, ἑαυτοὺς καὶ ἀλλήλους
καὶ πᾶσαν τὴν ζωὴν ἡμῶν Χριστῷ τῷ Θεῷ παραθώμεθα.
Λαός·

Σοί, Κύ - ρι - ε.
Si, Ki - ri - e.

> *Ἱερεύς (χαμηλοφώνως):* Κύριε ὁ Θεὸς ἡμῶν, σῶσον τὸν λαόν σου
> καὶ εὐλόγησον τὴν κληρονομίαν σου· τὸ πλήρωμα τῆς Ἐκκλησίας
> σου φύλαξον· ἁγίασον τοὺς ἀγαπῶντας τὴν εὐπρέπειαν τοῦ οἴκου
> σου· σὺ αὐτοὺς ἀντιδόξασον τῇ θεϊκῇ σου δυνάμει καὶ μὴ ἐγκατα-
> λίπῃς ἡμᾶς τοὺς ἐλπίζοντας ἐπὶ σέ.

Ἱερεύς· Ὅτι σὸν τὸ κράτος καὶ σοῦ ἐστιν ἡ βασιλεία καὶ ἡ δύναμις
καὶ ἡ δόξα τοῦ Πατρὸς καὶ τοῦ Υἱοῦ καὶ τοῦ Ἁγίου Πνεύματος,
νῦν καὶ ἀεὶ καὶ εἰς τοὺς αἰῶνας τῶν αἰώνων.
Λαός·

Ἀ - μήν.
A - min.

THE SHORT LITANY

Priest: In peace let us again pray to the Lord.
People:

Lord, have mer - cy.

Priest: Help us, save us, have mercy on us,
and protect us, O God, by Your grace.
People:

Lord, have mer - cy.

Priest:
Remembering our most holy, pure, blessed, and
glorious Lady, the Theotokos and ever virgin Mary,
with all the saints, let us commit ourselves, and
one another, and our whole life to Christ our God.
People:

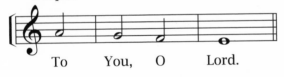

To You, O Lord.

Priest (in a low voice): Lord, our God, save Your people and bless
Your inheritance; protect the whole body of your Church, sanctify
those who love the beauty of Your house; glorify them in return
by Your divine power and do not forsake us who hope in You.

Priest: For Yours is the dominion, the kingdom, the
power and the glory, of the + Father and the Son and
the Holy Spirit, now and ever and to the ages of ages.
People:

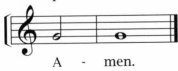

A - men.

ΤΟ ΔΕΥΤΕΡΟΝ ΑΝΤΙΦΩΝΟΝ

Καὶ ψάλλεται τὸ ἀντίφωνον, συνοδευόμενον ἀπὸ τὸ ἐφύμνιον.
Λαός·

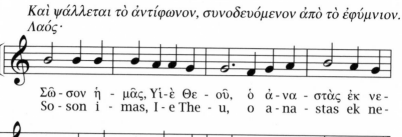

Σῶ - σον ἡ - μᾶς, Υἱ-ὲ Θε - οῦ, ὁ ἀ-να - στὰς ἐκ νε-
So - son i - mas, I - e The - u, o a - na - stas ek ne-

κρῶν, ψάλ - λον - τάς σοι· Ἀλ-λη-λού - ϊ - α.(3)
kron, psal - lon - das si: Al - li - lu - i - a.(3)

Εἰς τὰς καθημερινὰς ψάλλεται·

Σῶ-σον ἡ - μᾶς, Υἱ-ὲ Θε - οῦ, ὁ ἐν ἁ - γίοις θαυ-μα-
So - son i - mas, I - e The - u, o en a - gis thav-ma-

στός, ψάλ - λον - τάς σοι· Ἀλ-λη-λού-ϊ - α.(3)
stos, psal - lon - das si: Al - li - lu - i - a.(3)

Δό ξα Πατρὶ καὶ Υἱῷ καὶ Ἁγίῳ Πνεύ - μα - τι· καὶ
Thoxa Patri ke Io ke Ayio Pnev - ma - ti; ke

νῦν καὶ ἀεὶ καὶ εἰς τοὺς αἰῶνας τῶν αἰ - ώ - νων. Ἀ - μήν.
nin ke ai ke is tus eonas ton e - o - non. A - min.

THE SECOND ANTIPHON

The designated psalm verses are sung with the refrain.

On ordinary Sundays:

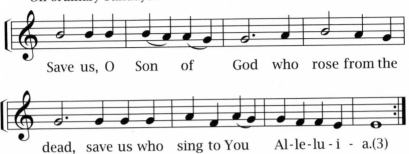

Save us, O Son of God who rose from the

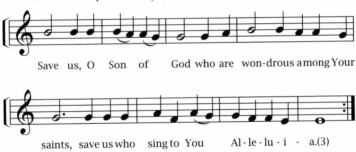

dead, save us who sing to You Al - le - lu - i - a.(3)

On ordinary weekdays, instead of the above:

Save us, O Son of God who are won-drous among Your

saints, save us who sing to You Al - le - lu - i - a.(3)

Some feast days have their own Second Antiphon.

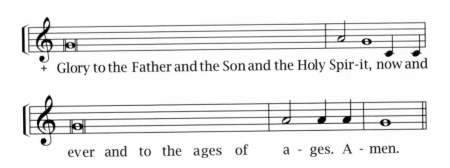

+ Glory to the Father and the Son and the Holy Spir-it, now and

ever and to the ages of a - ges. A - men.

'Ο μο-νο-γε - νὴς Υἱ-ὸς καὶ Λό-γος τοῦ Θε - οῦ ἀ -
O mo-no-ge - nis I - os ke Lo-gos tu The - u a -

θά - να - τος ὑ - πάρ - χων, καὶ κα - τα - δε - ξά - με - νος δι -
tha-na-tos i - par - hon, ke ka - ta - the - xa-me-nos thi -

ἀ τὴν ἡ - με - τέ - ραν σω - τη - ρί - αν σαρ - κω -
a tin i - me - ta - ran so - ti - ri - an sar - ko -

θῆ - ναι ἐκ τῆς ἁ - γί - ας Θε - ο - τό - κου
thi - ne ek tis a - gi - as The-o - to - ku

καὶ ἀ - ει - παρ - θέ - νου Μα - ρί - ας, ἀ -
ke a - i - par - the - nu Ma - ri - as, a -

τρέ - πτως ἐν - αν - θρω - πή - σας· σταυ - ρω -
trep - tos en - an - thro - pi - sas; stav - ro -

30

On - ly be - got-ten Son and Word of God, though im-mor - tal, for our sal - va - tion you deigned to be in - car - nate of the ho - ly The - o - to - kos and ev - er vir-gin Mar - y, with - out change be - com-ing man, and were cru - ci - fied, Christ our God, tramp-ling death by death; be - ing

θείς τε, Χρι - στὲ ὁ Θε - ός, θα -
this te, Hri - ste o The - os, tha -

νά - τῳ θά - να - τον πα - τή - σας· εἰς ὢν τῆς ᾿Α -
na - to tha - na - ton pa - ti - sas; is on tis A -

γί - ας Τρι - ά - δος, συν - δο - ξα -
gi - as Tri - a - thos, sin tho - xa -

ζό - με - νος τῷ Πα - τρὶ καὶ τῷ ᾿Α -
zo - me - nos to Pa - tri ke to A -

γί - ῳ Πνεύ - μα - τι, σῶ - σον ἡ - μᾶς.
gi - o Pnev - ma - ti, so - son i - mas.

one of the ho - ly Trin - i - ty,

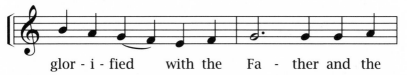

glor - i - fied with the Fa - ther and the

Ho - ly Spir - it: Save us.

Η ΜΙΚΡΑ ΣΥΝΑΠΤΗ

Ἱερεύς· Ἔτι καὶ ἔτι ἐν εἰρήνῃ τοῦ Κυρίου δεηθῶμεν.
Λαός·

Κύ - ρι - ε, ’λέ - η - σον.
Ki - ri - e, 'le - i - son.

Ἱερεύς· Ἀντιλαβοῦ, σῶσον, ἐλέησον καὶ
διαφύλαξον ἡμᾶς, ὁ Θεός, τῇ σῇ χάριτι.
Λαός·

Κύ - ρι - ε, ἐ - λέ - η - σον.
Ki - ri - e, e - le - i - son.

Ἱερεύς· Τῆς παναγίας, ἀχράντου, ὑπερευλογημένης, ἐνδόξου,
δεσποίνης ἡμῶν Θεοτόκου καὶ ἀειπαρθένου Μαρίας, μετὰ
πάντων τῶν ἁγίων μνημονεύσαντες, ἑαυτοὺς καὶ ἀλλήλους
καὶ πᾶσαν τὴν ζωὴν ἡμῶν Χριστῷ τῷ Θεῷ παραθώμεθα.
Λαός·

Σοί, Κύ - ρι - ε.
Si, Ki - ri - e.

Ἱερεύς (χαμηλοφώνως): Ὁ τὰς κοινὰς ταύτας καὶ συμφώνους
ἡμῖν χαρισάμενος προσευχάς, ὁ καὶ δυσὶ καὶ τρισὶ συμφωνοῦσιν
ἐπὶ τῷ ὀνόματί σου, τὰς αἰτήσεις παρέχειν ἐπαγγειλάμενος· αὐτὸς
καὶ νῦν τῶν δούλων σου τὰ αἰτήματα πρὸς τὸ συμφέρον πλήρωσον,
χορηγῶν ἡμῖν ἐν τῷ παρόντι αἰῶνι τὴν ἐπίγνωσιν τῆς σῆς ἀληθείας
καὶ ἐν τῷ μέλλοντι ζωὴν αἰώνιον χαριζόμενος.

Ἱερεύς· Ὅτι ἀγαθὸς φιλάνθρωπος Θεὸς ὑπάρχιες, καὶ σοὶ τὴν
δόξαν ἀναπέμπομεν, τῷ Πατρὶ καὶ τῷ Υἱῷ καὶ τῷ Ἁγίῳ Πνεύματι,
νῦν καὶ ἀεὶ καὶ εἰς τοὺς αἰῶνας τῶν αἰώνων.
Λαός·

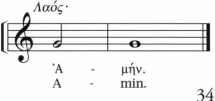

Ἀ - μήν.
A - min.

THE SHORT LITANY

Priest: In peace let us again pray to the Lord.
People:

Lord, have mer - cy.

Priest: Help us, save us, have mercy on us,
and protect us, O God, by Your grace.
People:

Lord, have mer - cy.

Priest:
Remembering our most holy, pure, blessed, and
glorious Lady, the Theotokos and ever virgin Mary,
with all the saints, let us commit ourselves, and
one another, and our whole life to Christ our God.
People:

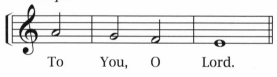

To You, O Lord.

Priest (in a low voice): Lord, You have given us grace to offer these
common prayers with one heart. You have promised to grant the
requests of two or three gathered in Your name. Fulfill now the
petitions of Your servants for our benefit, giving us the knowledge
of Your truth in this world and granting us everlasting life in the
world to come.

Priest: For You are a good and loving God and to You we
give glory, to the + Father and the Son and the Holy Spirit,
now and ever and to the ages of ages.
People:

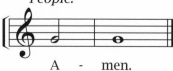

A - men.

35

ΤΟ ΤΡΙΤΟΝ ΑΝΤΙΦΩΝΟΝ

Καὶ ψάλλεται τὸ ἀντίφωνον, συνοδευόμενον ἀπὸ τὸ ἀπολυτίκιον.

Η ΜΙΚΡΑ ΕΙΣΟΔΟΣ

Ἱερεύς· Σοφία. Ὀρθοί.
Λαός·

Δεῦ - τε προ-σκυ - νή-σω-μεν καὶ προ - σπέ - σω - μεν Χρι-
Thev- te pro- ski - ni- so-men ke pro - spe - so - men Hri-

στῷ.
sto.

Σῶ- σον ἡ - μᾶς, Υἱ-ὲ Θε-
So - son i - mas, I - e The-

οῦ, ὁ ἀ - να - στὰς ἐκ νε - κρῶν,
u, o a - na - stas ek ne - kron,

(ὁ ἐν ἁ - γίοις θαυ - μα - στός,)
(o en a - gis thav - ma - stos,)

ψάλ - λον - τάς σοι· Ἀλ - λη - λού - ϊ - α.
psal - lon - das si: Al - li - lu - i - a.

Τελεῖται ἡ Μικρὰ Εἴσοδος παρὰ τοῦ ἱερατείου.
Ἐπαναλαμβάνεται τὸ ἀπολυτίκιον μετὰ τοῦ κοντακίου.

THE THIRD ANTIPHON

The designated psalm verses are sung with the apolitikion.

*On ordinary Sundays we sing the resurrectional apolitikion
of the tone of the week. See pages 98-127.
During the Paschal season we sing Χριστὸς ἀνέστη/Christ is risen,
pages 152/153. On greater feasts we sing the apolitikion of the
feast. See pages 128-223.*

THE ENTRANCE

Priest: Wisdom. Let us be attentive.
On ordinary Sundays we sing:

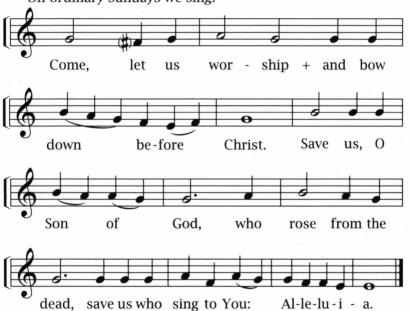

Come, let us wor - ship + and bow

down be-fore Christ. Save us, O

Son of God, who rose from the

dead, save us who sing to You: Al-le-lu-i - a.

*On great feasts and during the Paschal season we sing the
proper entrance hymn instead of the above. We conclude
the hymn as in the refrain of the Second Antiphon of the day.*

*The clergy make the entrance. We repeat the apolitikion,
any other designated apolitikia, and end with the kontakion.
See pages 224-289.*

37

Ο ΤΡΙΣΑΓΙΟΣ ΥΜΝΟΣ

Ἱερεύς· Τοῦ Κυρίου δεηθῶμεν.
Λαός·

Κύ - ρι - ε, ᾿λέ - η - σον.
Ki - ri - e, 'le - i - son.

Ἱερεύς· ῞Οτι ἅγιος εἶ ὁ Θεὸς ἡμῶν, καὶ σοὶ τὴν δόξαν
ἀναπέμπομεν, τῷ Πατρὶ καὶ τῷ Υἱῷ καὶ τῷ ῾Αγίῳ
Πνεύματι, νῦν καὶ ἀεὶ καὶ εἰς τοὺς αἰῶνας τῶν αἰώνων.
Λαός·

᾿Α - μην.
A - min.

῞Α - γι - ος ὁ Θε - ός, ἅ - γι - ος ᾿Ισ - χυ - ρός,
A - gi - os o The - os, a - gi - os Is - hi - ros,

ἅ - γι - ος ᾿Α - θά - να - τος, ἐ - λέ - η - σον ἡ - μᾶς.(3)
a - gi - os A - tha - na - tos, e - le - i - son i - mas.(3)

Δό - ξα Πα - τρὶ καὶ Υἱ - ῷ καὶ ῾Α - γί - ῳ Πνεύ - μα - τι· καὶ
Tho - xa Pa - tri ke I - o ke A - gi - o Pnev - ma - ti; ke

νῦν καὶ ἀ - εὶ καὶ εἰς τοὺς αἰ - ῶ - νας τῶν αἰ - ώ - νων. ᾿Α - μήν.
nin ke a - i ke is tus e - o - nas ton e - o - non. A - min.

38

THE TRISAGION HYMN

Priest: Let us pray to the Lord.
People:

Lord, have mer - cy.

Priest: For You are holy, our God, and to You we give glory, to the + Father and the Son and the Holy Spirit, now and ever and to the ages of ages.
People:

A - men.

On some feast days we sing a different hymn. See pages 290-293.

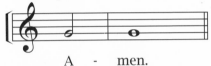

+ Ho - ly God, ho - ly Might - y,

ho - ly Im - mor - tal, have mer - cy on us.(3)

+ Glory to the Father and the Son and the Holy Spir-it,

now and ever and to the ages of a - ges. A - men.

This hymn is continued on pages 40/41.

"Α - γι-ος 'Α - θά - να - τος, ἐ - λέ - η - σον ἡ - μᾶς.
A - gi-os A - tha - na - tos, e - le - i - son i - mas.

Ἱερεύς· Δύναμις.
Λαός·

"Α - γι - ος ὁ Θε - ός, ἅ - γι - ος 'Iσ - χυ - ρός,
A - gi - os o The - os, a - gi - os Is - hi - ros,

ἅ - γι-ος 'Α - θά - να - τος, ἐ - λέ - η - σον ἡ - μᾶς.
a - gi-os A - tha - na - tos, e - le - i - son i - mas.

Ο ΑΠΟΣΤΟΛΟΣ

Ἱερεύς· Πρόσχωμεν.
Ὁ Ἀναγνώστης ἐκφωνεῖ τοὺς στίχους τῶν ψαλμῶν.
Ἱερεύς· Σοφία. Πρόσχωμεν.
Ὁ Ἀναγνώστης ἀναγινώσκει τὴν τεταγμένην ἀποστολικήν
περικοπήν.

Ἱερεύς (χαμηλοφώνως): "Ἔλλαμψον ἐν ταῖς καρδίαις ἡμῶν,
φιλάνθρωπε Δέσποτα, τὸ τῆς σῆς θεογνωσίας ἀκήρατον φῶς
καὶ τοὺς τῆς διανοίας ἡμῶν διάνοιξον ὀφθαλμοὺς εἰς τὴν τῶν
εὐαγγελικῶν σου κηρυγμάτων κατανόησιν. "Ἔνθες ἡμῖν καὶ τὸν
τῶν μακαρίων σου ἐντολῶν φόβον, ἵνα, τὰς σαρκικὰς ἐπιθυμίας
πάσας καταπατήσαντες, πνευματικὴν πολιτείαν μετέλθωμεν, πάντα
τὰ πρὸς εὐαρέστησιν τὴν σὴν καὶ φρονοῦντες καὶ πράττοντες.

Σὺ γὰρ εἶ ὁ φωτισμὸς τῶν ψυχῶν καὶ τῶν σωμάτων ἡμῶν, Χριστὲ
ὁ Θεός, καὶ σοὶ τὴν δόξαν ἀναπέμπομεν σὺν τῷ ἀνάρχῳ σου
Πατρὶ καὶ τῷ παναγίῳ καὶ ἀγαθῷ καὶ ζωοποιῷ σου Πνεύματι,
νῦν καὶ ἀεὶ καὶ εἰς τοὺς αἰῶνας τῶν αἰώνων. Ἀμήν.

Ho - ly Im-mor - tal, have mer - cy on us.

Priest: Again, fervently.
People:

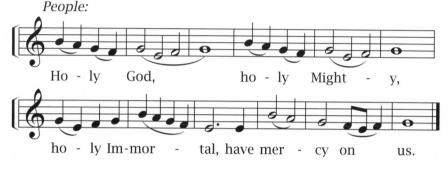

Ho - ly God, ho - ly Might - y,

ho - ly Im-mor - tal, have mer - cy on us.

THE EPISTLE

Priest: Let us be attentive.
The reader reads the prokimenon, verses from the psalms.
Priest: Wisdom. Let us be attentive.
The Reader reads the designated Apostolic pericope.

Priest (in a low voice): Shine within our hearts, loving Master, the pure light of Your divine knowledge, and open the eyes of our minds that we may comprehend the message of Your Gospel. Instill in us also reverence for Your blessed commandments so that, having conquered sinful desires, we may pursue a spiritual life, thinking and doing all those things which are pleasing to You.

For You, Christ our God, are the light of our souls and bodies, and to You we give glory, together with Your Father who is without beginning and Your all holy, good and life giving Spirit, now and ever and to the ages of ages. Amen.

Ἱερεύς· Εἰρήνη σοι.

ΤΟ ΙΕΡΟΝ ΕΥΑΓΓΕΛΙΟΝ

Ἱερεύς· Σοφία. Ὀρθοί. Ἀκούσωμεν τοῦ ἁγίου Εὐαγγελίου.
Εἰρήνη πᾶσι.

Ἱερεύς· Ἐκ τοῦ κατὰ (ὄνομα) ἁγίου Εὐαγγελίου τὸ ἀνάγνωσμα.
Πρόσχωμεν.

Ὁ Ἱερεύς ἀναγινώσκει τὴν τεταγμένην περικοπήν τοῦ
ἁγίου Εὐαγγελίου.
Λαός· **Δόξα σοι, Κύριε, δόξα σοι.**

42

The priest blesses the reader, saying: Peace be with you.

THE GOSPEL

People:

Al - le - lu - i - a, al-le - lu - i - a, al - le - lu - i - a.

Priest: Wisdom. Arise. Let us hear the holy Gospel.
Peace be with all.
People:

And with your spir - it.

Priest: The reading is from the holy Gospel according
to *(name).* Let us be attentive.
People:

Glo - ry to You, O Lord, glo - ry to You.

*The Priest reads the designated pericope of the holy Gospel.
At the conclusion of the Gospel reading we sing again:*
Glory to You, O Lord, glory to You.

ΧΕΡΟΥΒΙΚΟΝ

Ἱερεύς· ῞Οπως ὑπὸ τοῦ κράτους σου πάντοτε φυλαττόμενοι, σοὶ
δόξαν ἀναπέμπωμεν, τῷ Πατρὶ καὶ τῷ Υἱῷ καὶ τῷ ᾿Αγίῳ Πνεύματι,
νῦν καὶ ἀεὶ καὶ εἰς τοὺς αἰῶνας τῶν αἰώνων.
Λαός·

᾿Α - μήν. Οἱ τὰ χε - ρου - βεὶμ,
A - min. I ta he - ru - vim,

οἱ τὰ χε-ρου - βεὶμ μυ - στι - κῶς εἰ - κο -
i ta he-ru - vim mi - sti - kos i - ko -

νί - ζον - τες
ni - zon - des

καὶ τῇ ζω - ο - ποι -
ke ti zo - o - pi -

ῷ Τρι - ά -
o Tri - a -

δι, Τρι - ά - δι τὸν τρι -
thi, Tri - a - thi ton tri -

44

THE CHERUBIC HYMN

Priest: And grant that always guarded by Your power we may give glory to You, the + Father and the Son and the Holy Spirit, now and ever and to the ages of ages.
People:

A - men.   Let   us who   mys - tic' - lly

re - pre - sent the che - ru - bim,   re - pre-

sent   the   che - ru - bim,

let us who mys - tic'-lly re - pre - sent   the

che - ru - bim and sing   the

thrice   ho - ly   hymn to the   life

giv-ing Tri - ni-ty, set a - side   all cares,

For an alternate Cherubic Hymn see pages 294/295.

all   cares, all   cares of   life.

Let us set a - side   all   cares of life. Let us

set   a - side all   cares   of   life.

Let   us   set   a-side   all   cares of life

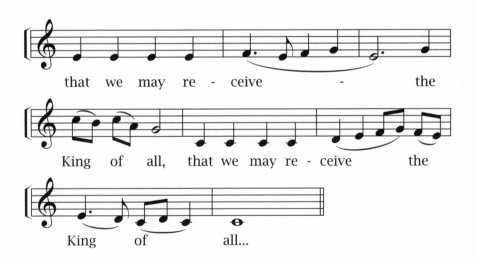

that we may re - ceive   -   the

King   of   all,   that we may re - ceive   the

King   of   all...

Ἰερεύς· Πάντων ὑμῶν μνησθείη Κύριος ὁ Θεὸς ἐν τῇ βασιλείᾳ αὐτοῦ πάντοτε, νῦν καὶ ἀεὶ καὶ εἰς τοὺς αἰῶνας τῶν αἰώνων.
Λαός·

Ἀ - μήν.
A - min.

Ὁ Ἰερεύς εἰσέρχεται εἰς τὸ Ἰερὸν Βῆμα, ὁ δὲ λαὸς ψάλλει τὸ τέλος τοῦ Χερουβικοῦ·

Ταῖς ἀγ - γε - λι - καῖς ἀ - ο - ρά - τως δο - ρυ - φο -
Tes an - ge - li - kes a - o - ra - tos tho - ri - fo -

ρού - με - νον τά - ξε - σιν,
ru - me - non ta - xe - sin,

τά - ξε - σιν. Ἀλ - λη - λού - ϊ -
ta - xe - sin. Al - li - lu - i -

α, ἀλ - λη - λού - ϊ - α, ἀλ - λη -
a, al - li - lu - i - a, al - li -

λού - ϊ - α.
lu - i - a.

48

Priest: May the Lord God remember + all of you in His kingdom, now and ever and to the ages of ages.
People:

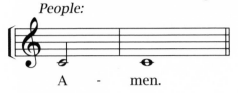

A - men.

The priest enters the sanctuary while the people sing the end of the Cherubic Hymn:

In - vis - i - bly es - cor - ted, es - cor - ted

by the an - ge - lic hosts, by the an -

ge - lic hosts, by an - ge - lic hosts. Al - le -

lu - i - a, al - le - lu - i -

a, al - le - lu - i - a.

ΤΑ ΠΛΗΡΩΤΙΚΑ

Ἱερεύς· Πληρώσωμεν τὴν δέησιν ἡμῶν τῷ Κυρίῳ.
Λαός·

Κύ - ρι - ε, 'λέ - η - σον.
Ki - ri - e, 'le - i - son.

Ἱερεύς· Ὑπὲρ τῶν προτεθέντων τιμίων
δώρων, τοῦ Κυρίου δεηθῶμεν.
Λαός·

Κύ - ρι - ε, ἐ - λέ - η - σον.
Ki - ri - e, e - le - i - son.

Ἱερεύς· Ὑπὲρ τοῦ ἁγίου οἴκου τούτου καὶ τῶν μετὰ πίστεως,
εὐλαβείας καὶ φόβου Θεοῦ εἰσιόντων ἐν αὐτῷ, τοῦ Κυρίου δεηθῶμεν.
Λαός·

Κύ - ρι - ε, ἐ - λέ - η - σον.
Ki - ri - e, e - le - i - son.

Ἱερεύς· Ὑπὲρ τοῦ ῥυσθῆναι ἡμᾶς ἀπὸ πάσης θλίψεως,
ὀργῆς, κινδύνου καὶ ἀνάγκης, τοῦ Κυρίου δεηθῶμεν.
Λαός·

Κύ - ρι - ε, 'λέ - η - σον.
Ki - ri - e, 'le - i - son.

THE PETITIONS

Priest: Let us complete our prayer to the Lord.
People:

Lord, have mer - cy.

Priest: For the precious gifts here presented,
let us pray to the Lord.
People:

Lord, have mer - cy.

Priest: For this holy house and for those who enter it with
faith, reverence and the fear of God, let us pray to the Lord.
People:

Lord, have mer - cy.

Priest: For our deliverance from all affliction, wrath,
danger and distress, let us pray to the Lord.
People:

Lord, have mer - cy.

Ἱερεύς· Ἀντιλαβοῦ, σῶσον, ἐλέησον καὶ διαφύλαξον ἡμᾶς, ὁ Θεός, τῇ σῇ χάριτι.
Λαός·

Κύ - ρι - ε, ἐ - λέ - η - σον.
Ki - ri - e, e - le - i - son.

Ἱερεύς· Τὴν ἡμέραν πᾶσαν τελείαν, ἀγίαν, εἰρηνικὴν καὶ ἀναμάρτητον, παρὰ τοῦ Κυρίου αἰτησώμεθα.
Λαός·

Πα - ράσ-χου, Κύ - ρι - ε.
Pa - ras - hu, Ki - ri - e.

Ἱερεύς· Ἄγγελου εἰρήνης, πιστὸν ὁδηγόν, φύλακα τῶν ψυχῶν καὶ τῶν σωμάτων ἡμῶν, παρὰ τοῦ Κυρίου αἰτησώμεθα.
Λαός·

Πα - ράσ-χου, Κύ - ρι - ε.
Pa - ras - hu, Ki - ri - e.

Ἱερεύς· Συγγνώμην καὶ ἄφεσιν τῶν ἁμαρτιῶν καὶ τῶν πλημμελημάτων ἡμῶν, παρὰ τοῦ Κυρίου αἰτησώμεθα.
Λαός·

Πα - ράσ-χου, Κύ - ρι - ε.
Pa - ras - hu, Ki - ri - e.

Ἱερεύς· Τὰ καλὰ καὶ συμφέροντα ταῖς ψυχαῖς ἡμῶν καὶ εἰρήνην τῷ κόσμῳ, παρὰ τοῦ Κυρίου αἰτησώμεθα.
Λαός·

Πα - ράσ-χου, Κύ - ρι - ε.
Pa - ras - hu, Ki - ri - e.

Priest: Help us, save us, have mercy upon us
and protect us, O God, by Your grace.
People:

Lord, have mer - cy.

Priest: For a perfect, holy, peaceful and sinless day,
let us ask the Lord.
People:

Grant this, O Lord.

Priest: For an angel of peace, a faithful guide, a guardian
of our souls and bodies, let us ask the Lord.
People:

Grant this, O Lord.

Priest: For forgiveness and remission of our
sins and transgressions, let us ask the Lord.
People:

Grant this, O Lord.

Priest: For all that is good and beneficial to our souls,
and for peace in the world, let us ask the Lord.
People:

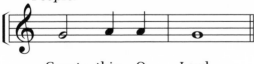

Grant this, O Lord.

Ἱερεύς· Τὸν ὑπόλοιπον χρόνον τῆς ζωῆς ἡμῶν, ἐν εἰρήνῃ καὶ μετανοίᾳ ἐκτελέσαι, παρὰ τοῦ Κυρίου αἰτησώμεθα.

Λαός·

Πα - ράσ-χου, Κύ - ρι - ε.
Pa - ras - hu, Ki - ri - e.

Ἱερεύς· Χριστιανὰ τὰ τέλη τῆς ζωῆς ἡμῶν, ἀνώδυνα, ἀνεπαίσχυντα, εἰρηνικὰ καὶ καλὴν ἀπολογίαν τὴν ἐπὶ τοῦ φοβεροῦ βήματος τοῦ Χριστοῦ αἰτησώμεθα.

Λαός·

Πα - ράσ-χου, Κύ - ρι - ε.
Pa - ras - hu, Ki - ri - e.

Ἱερεύς· Τῆς παναγίας, ἀχράντου, ὑπερευλογημένης, ἐνδόξου δεσποίνης ἡμῶν Θεοτόκου καὶ ἀειπαρθένου Μαρίας, μετὰ πάντων τῶν ἁγίων μνημονεύσαντες, ἑαυτοὺς καὶ ἀλλήλους καὶ πᾶσαν τὴν ζωὴν ἡμῶν Χριστῷ τῷ Θεῷ παραθώμεθα.

Λαός·

Σοί, Κύ - ρι - ε.
Si, Ki - ri - e.

Ἱερεύς· Διὰ τῶν οἰκτιρμῶν τοῦ μονογενοῦς σου Υἱοῦ, μεθ' οὗ εὐλογητὸς εἶ, σὺν τῷ πα- ναγίῳ καὶ ἀγαθῷ καὶ ζωοποιῷ σου Πνεύματι, νῦν καὶ ἀεὶ καὶ εἰς τοὺς αἰῶνας τῶν αἰώνων.

Λαός·

Ἀ - μήν.
A - min.

Priest: For the completion of our lives in peace and repentance, let us ask the Lord.
People:

Grant this, O Lord.

Priest: For a Christian end to our lives, peaceful, without shame and suffering, and for a good account before the awesome judgment seat of Christ, let us ask the Lord.
People:

Grant this, O Lord.

Priest: Remembering + our most holy, pure, blessed, and glorious Lady, the Theotokos and ever virgin Mary, with all the saints, let us commit ourselves, and one another, and our whole life to Christ our God.
People:

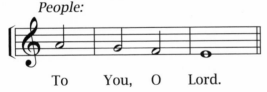

To You, O Lord.

Priest: Through the mercies of Your only begotten Son, with whom You are blessed together with Your all holy, good, and life giving Spirit, now and ever and to the ages of ages.
People:

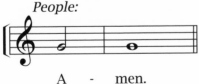

A - men.

Ἱερεύς· Εἰρήνη πᾶσι.
Λαός·

Καὶ τῷ πνεύ - μα - τί σου.
Ke to pnev - ma - ti su.

Ἱερεύς· Ἀγαπήσωμεν ἀλλήλους, ἵνα ἐν ὁμονοίᾳ ὁμολογήσωμεν.
Λαός·

Πα - τέ - ρα, Υἱ - όν καὶ Ἅ - γι - ον
Pa - te - ra, I - on ke A - gi - on

Πνεῦ - μα, Τρι - ά - δα ὁ - μο - ού - σι -
Pnev - ma, Tri - a - tha o - mo - u - si -

ον καὶ ἀ - χώ - ρι - στον.
on ke a - ho - ri - ston.

Ἱερεύς· Τὰς θύρας, τὰς θύρας, ἐν σοφίᾳ πρόσχωμεν.

Priest: Peace be with all.
People:

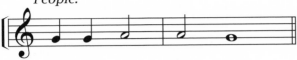

And with your spi - rit.

Priest: Let us love one another that with one mind we may confess:
People:

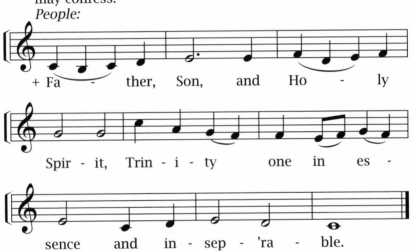

+ Fa - ther, Son, and Ho - ly

Spir - it, Trin - i - ty one in es -

sence and in - sep - 'ra - ble.

Priest: Guard the doors. Wisdom. Let us be attentive.

ΤΟ ΣΥΜΒΟΛΟΝ ΤΗΣ ΠΙΣΤΕΩΣ

Ἱερεύς καὶ Λαός·
Πιστεύω εἰς ἕνα Θεόν, Πατέρα, παντοκράτορα, ποιητὴν
οὐρανοῦ καὶ γῆς, ὁρατῶν τε πάντων καὶ ἀοράτων.

Καὶ εἰς ἕνα Κύριον, Ἰησοῦν Χριστόν, τὸν Υἱὸν τοῦ Θεοῦ τὸν
μονογενῆ, τὸν ἐκ τοῦ Πατρὸς γεννηθέντα πρὸ πάντων τῶν
αἰώνων. Φῶς ἐκ φωτός, Θεὸν ἀληθινὸν ἐκ Θεοῦ ἀληθινοῦ,
γεννηθέντα, οὐ ποιηθέντα, ὁμοούσιον τῷ Πατρί, δι' οὗ τὰ
πάντα ἐγένετο.

Τὸν δι' ἡμᾶς τοὺς ἀνθρώπους καὶ διὰ τὴν ἡμετέραν σωτηρίαν
κατελθόντα ἐκ τῶν οὐρανῶν καὶ σαρκωθέντα ἐκ Πνεύματος
Ἁγίου καὶ Μαρίας τῆς Παρθένου καὶ ἐνανθρωπήσαντα.

Σταυρωθέντα τε ὑπὲρ ἡμῶν ἐπὶ Ποντίου Πιλάτου καὶ παθόντα
καὶ ταφέντα.

Καὶ ἀναστάντα τῇ τρίτῃ ἡμέρᾳ κατὰ τὰς Γραφάς.
Καὶ ἀνελθόντα εἰς τοὺς οὐρανοὺς καὶ καθεζόμενον ἐκ δεξιῶν
τοῦ Πατρός.

Καὶ πάλιν ἐρχόμενον μετὰ δόξης κρῖναι ζῶντας καὶ νεκρούς,
οὗ τῆς βασιλείας οὐκ ἔσται τέλος.

Καὶ εἰς τὸ Πνεῦμα τὸ Ἅγιον, τὸ Κύριον, τὸ ζωοποιόν, τὸ ἐκ τοῦ
Πατρὸς ἐκπορευόμενον, τὸ σὺν Πατρὶ καὶ Υἱῷ
συμπροσκυνούμενον καὶ συνδοξαζόμενον, τὸ λαλῆσαν διὰ
τῶν Προφητῶν.

Εἰς μίαν, ἁγίαν, καθολικὴν καὶ ἀποστολικὴν Ἐκκλησίαν.

Ὁμολογῶ ἓν βάπτισμα εἰς ἄφεσιν ἁμαρτιῶν.
Προσδοκῶ ἀνάστασιν νεκρῶν.
Καὶ ζωὴν τοῦ μέλλοντος αἰῶνος. Ἀμήν.

The Confession of Faith

I BELIEVE in one God, Father Almighty, Creator of heaven and earth, and of all things visible and invisible.

And in one Lord Jesus Christ, the only-begotten Son of God, begotten of the Father before all ages; Light of Light, true God of true God, begotten, not created, of one essence with the Father, through Whom all things were made.

Who for us men and for our salvation came down from heaven and was incarnate of the Holy Spirit and the Virgin Mary and became man.

He was crucified for us under Pontius Pilate, and suffered and was buried;

And He rose on the third day, according to the Scriptures.

He ascended into heaven and is seated at the right hand of the Father;

And He will come again with glory to judge the living and the dead; His kingdom shall have no end.

And in the Holy Spirit, the Lord, the Creator of Life, Who proceeds from the Father, Who together with the Father and the Son is worshipped and glorified, Who spoke through the prophets.

In one holy, catholic, and apostolic Church.

I confess one baptism for the forgiveness of sins.

I look for the resurrection of the dead, and the life of the age to come.

AMEN

Η ΑΓΙΑ ΑΝΑΦΟΡΑ

Ἱερεύς· Στῶμεν καλῶς· στῶμεν μετὰ φόβου· πρόσχωμεν· τὴν ἁγίαν ἀναφορὰν ἐν εἰρήνῃ προσφέρειν.
Λαός·

Ἔ-λε-ον εἰ-ρή-νης, θυ-σί-αν αἰ-νέ-σε-ως.
E - le - on i - ri - nis, thi - si - an e - ne-se - os.

Ἱερεύς· Ἡ χάρις τοῦ Κυρίου ἡμῶν Ἰησοῦ Χριστοῦ καὶ ἡ ἀγάπη τοῦ Θεοῦ καὶ Πατρὸς καὶ ἡ κοινωνία τοῦ ἁγίου Πνεύματος, εἴη μετὰ πάντων ὑμῶν.
Λαός·

Καὶ με-τὰ τοῦ πνεύ-μα-τός σου.
Ke me-ta tu pnev-ma-tos su.

Ἱερεύς· Ἄνω σηῶμεν τὰς καρδίας.
Λαός·

Ἔ - χο-μεν πρὸς τὸν Κύ - ρι - ον.
E - ho-men pros ton Ki - ri - on.

Ἱερεύς· Εὐχαριστήσωμεν τῷ Κυρίῳ.
Λαός·

Ἄ - ξι - ον καὶ δί - και - ον.
A - xi - on ke thi - ke - on.

60

THE HOLY ANAPHORA

Priest: Let us stand well. Let us stand in awe. Let us be attentive that we may make the holy offering in peace.
People:

Mer - cy and peace, a sac-ri-fice of praise.

Priest: The grace of our Lord Jesus Christ, the love of God the Father, and the communion of the Holy Spirit be with all of you.
People:

And with your spir - it.

Priest: Let us lift up our hearts.
People:

We lift them up to the Lord.

Priest: Let us give thanks to the Lord.
People:

It is pro-per and right.

Ἱερεύς (χαμηλοφώνως): Ἄξιον καὶ δίκαιον σὲ ὑμνεῖν, σὲ εὐλογεῖν, σὲ αἰνεῖν, σοὶ εὐχαριστεῖν, σὲ προσκυνεῖν ἐν παντὶ τόπῳ τῆς δεσποτείας σου. Σὺ γὰρ εἶ Θεὸς ἀνέκφραστος, ἀπερινόητος, ἀόρατος, ἀκατάληπτος, ἀεὶ ὤν, ὡσαύτως ὤν, σὺ καὶ ὁ μονογενής σου Υἱὸς καὶ τὸ Πνεῦμα σου τὸ Ἅγιον. Σὺ ἐκ τοῦ μὴ ὄντος εἰς τὸ εἶναι ἡμᾶς παρήγαγες, καὶ παραπεσόντας ἀνέστησας πάλιν, καὶ οὐκ ἀπέστης πάντα ποιῶν, ἕως ἡμᾶς εἰς τὸν οὐρανὸν ἀνήγαγες καὶ τὴν βασιλείαν σου ἐχαρίσω τὴν μέλλουσαν. Ὑπὲρ τούτων ἁπάντων εὐχαριστοῦμέν σοι καὶ τῷ μονογενεῖ σου Υἱῷ καὶ τῷ Πνεύματί σου τῷ Ἁγίῳ, ὑπὲρ πάντων ὧν ἴσμεν καὶ ὧν οὐκ ἴσμεν, τῶν φανερῶν καὶ ἀφανῶν εὐεργεσιῶν, τῶν εἰς ἡμᾶς γεγενημένων. Εὐχαριστοῦμεν σοι καὶ ὑπὲρ τῆς λειτουργίας ταύτης, ἣν ἐκ τῶν χειρῶν ἡμῶν δέξασθαι κατηξίωσας, καίτοι σοι παρεστήκασι χιλιάδες ἀρχαγγέλων καὶ μυριάδες ἀγγέλων, τὰ Χερουβεὶμ καὶ τὰ Σεραφείμ, ἑξαπτέρυγα, πολυόμματα, μετάρσια πτερωτά,

Ἱερεύς· Τὸν ἐπινίκιον ὕμνον ᾄδοντα, βοῶντα, κεκραγότα καὶ λέγοντα·

Λαός·

Ἅ - γι - ος, ἅ - γι - ος, ἅ - γι - ος, Κύ - ρι - ος Σα - βα - ώθ·
A - yi - os, a - yi - os, a - yi - os, Ki - ri - os Sa - va - oth;

πλή - ρης ὁ οὐ - ρα - νὸς καὶ ἡ γῆ τῆς δό - ξης σου. Ὡ - σαν -
pli - ris o u - ra - nos ke i yi tis tho - xis su. O - san -

νὰ ἐν τοῖς ὑ - ψί - στοις· εὐ - λο - γη - μέ - νος ὁ ἐρ -
na en tis i - psi - stis; ev - lo - yi - me - nos o er -

χό - με - νος ἐν ὀ - νό - μα - τι Κυ - ρί - ου.
ho - me - nos en o - no - ma - ti Ki - ri - u.

62

Priest (in a low voice): It is proper and right to sing to You, bless You, praise You, thank You and worship You in all places of Your dominion; for You are God ineffable, beyond comprehension, invisible, beyond understanding, existing forever and always the same; You and Your only begotten Son and Your Holy Spirit. You brought us into being out of nothing, and when we fell, You raised us up again. You did not cease doing everything until You led us to heaven and granted us Your kingdom to come. For all these things we thank You and Your only begotten Son and Your Holy Spirit; for all things that we know and do not know, for blessings seen and unseen that have been bestowed upon us. We also thank You for this liturgy which You are pleased to accept from our hands, even though You are surrounded by thousands of Archangels and tens of thousands of Angels, by the Cherubim and Seraphim, six-winged, many-eyed, soaring with their wings,

Priest: Singing the victory hymn, proclaiming, crying out and saying:
People:

Ho - ly, ho - ly, ho - ly Lord of Sa - ba - oth, heav - en, heav'n and earth are filled with Your glo - ry. Ho - san - na in the high - est. Bless - ed is He who comes in the name of the Lord. Ho - san -

'Ω-σαν - νά   ὁ ἐν τοῖς ὑ - ψί - στοις.
O - san - na   o en tis i - psi - stis.

Ἱερεύς (χαμηλοφώνως): Μετὰ τούτων καὶ ἡμεῖς τῶν μακαρίων δυνάμεων, Δέσποτα φιλάνθρωπε, βοῶμεν καὶ λέγομεν· Ἅγιος εἶ καὶ πανάγιος, Σὺ καὶ ὁ μονογενής σου Υἱός, καὶ τὸ Πνεῦμα σου τὸ Ἅγιον. Ἅγιος εἶ καὶ πανάγιος καὶ μεγαλοπρεπὴς ἡ δόξα σου· ὃς τὸν κόσμον σου οὕτως ἠγάπησας, ὥστε τὸν Υἱόν σου τὸν μονο- γενῆ δοῦναι, ἵνα πᾶς ὁ πιστεύων εἰς αὐτὸν μὴ ἀπόληται, ἀλλ' ἔχῃ ζωὴν αἰώνιον. Ὃς ἐλθὼν καὶ πᾶσαν τὴν ὑπὲρ ἡμῶν κληρονομίαν πληρώσας, τῇ νυκτὶ ᾗ παρεδίδετο, μᾶλλον δὲ ἑαυτὸν παρεδίδου ὑπὲρ τῆς τοῦ κόσμου ζωῆς, λαβὼν ἄρτον ἐν ταῖς ἁγίαις αὐτοῦ καὶ ἀχράντοις καὶ ἀμωμήτοις χερσίν, εὐχαριστήσας καὶ εὐλογή- σας, ἁγιάσας, κλάσας, ἔδωκε τοῖς ἁγίοις αὐτοῦ μαθηταῖς καὶ ἀπο- στόλοις, εἰπών·

Ἱερεύς· Λάβετε, φάγετε· τοῦτό μού ἐστι τὸ Σῶμα, τὸ ὑπὲρ ὑμῶν κλώμενον εἰς ἄφεσιν ἁμαρτιῶν.
Λαός·

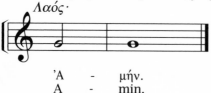

'Α - μήν.
A - min.

Ἱερεύς (χαμηλοφώνως): Ὁμοίως καὶ τὸ ποτήριον μετὰ τὸ δειπνῆσαι λέγων·

Ἱερεύς· Πίετε ἐξ αὐτοῦ πάντες· τοῦτό ἐστι τὸ Αἷμά μου, τὸ τῆς καινῆς Διαθήκης, τὸ ὑπὲρ ὑμῶν καὶ πολλῶν ἐκχυνόμενον εἰς ἄφεσιν ἁμαρτιῶν.
Λαός·

'Α - μήν.
A - min.

na,   ho - san - na   in   the   high - est.

> *Priest (in a low voice)*: Together with these blessed powers, merciful Master, we also proclaim and say: You are holy and most holy, You and Your only begotten Son and Your Holy Spirit. You are holy and most holy, and sublime is Your glory. You so loved Your world that You gave Your only begotten Son so that whoever believes in Him should not perish, but have eternal life. He came and fulfilled the divine plan for us. On the night when He was betrayed, or rather when He gave Himself up for the life of the world, He took bread in His holy, pure, and blameless hands, gave thanks, blessed, sanctified, broke, and gave it to His holy disciples and apostles saying:

Priest: Take, eat, this is my Body + which is
broken for you for the forgiveness of sins.
People:

A -   men.

> *Priest (in a low voice)*: Likewise, after supper, He took the cup, saying:

Priest: Drink of it all of you;
this is my Blood of the new Covenant
which is shed for you and for many
for the forgiveness of sins.
People:

A   -   men.

Ἱερεύς (χαμηλοφώνως): Μεμνημένοι τοίνυν τῆς σωτηρίου ταύτης ἐντολῆς καὶ πάντων τῶν ὑπὲρ ἡμῶν γεγενημένων, τοῦ σταυροῦ, τοῦ τάφου, τῆς τριημέρου ἀναστάσεως, τῆς εἰς οὐρανοὺς ἀναβάσεως, τῆς ἐκ δεξιῶν καθέδρας, τῆς δευτέρας καὶ ἐνδόξου πάλιν παρουσίας.

Ἱερεύς· Τὰ σὰ ἐκ τῶν σῶν σοὶ προσφέρομεν κατὰ πάντα καὶ διὰ πάντα.

Ἱερεύς (χαμηλοφώνως): Ἔτι προσφέρομέν σοι τὴν λογικὴν ταύτην καὶ ἀναίμακτον λατρείαν καὶ παρακαλοῦμέν σε καὶ δεόμεθα καὶ ἱκετεύομεν. Κατάπεμψον τὸ Πνεῦμά σου τὸ Ἅγιον ἐφ᾽ ἡμᾶς καὶ ἐπὶ τὰ προκείμενα δῶρα ταῦτα.

Καὶ ποίησον τὸν μὲν ἄρτον τοῦτον, τίμιον Σῶμα τοῦ Χριστοῦ σου. Ἀμήν.

Τὸ δὲ ἐν τῷ ποτηρίῳ τούτῳ, τίμιον Αἷμα τοῦ Χριστοῦ σου. Ἀμήν.

Μεταβαλὼν τῷ Πνεύματί σου τῷ Ἁγίῳ. Ἀμήν. Ἀμήν. Ἀμήν.

Λαός·

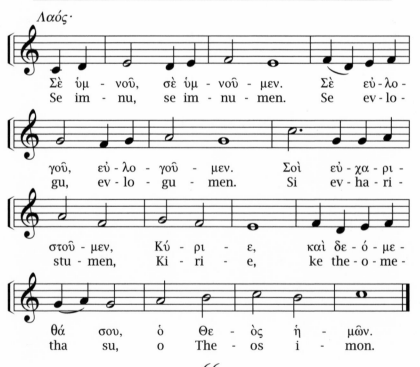

Σὲ ὑμ - νοῦ, σὲ ὑμ - νοῦ - μεν. Σὲ εὐ - λο -
Se im - nu, se im - nu - men. Se ev - lo -

γοῦ, εὐ - λο - γοῦ - μεν. Σοὶ εὐ - χα - ρι -
gu, ev - lo - gu - men. Si ev - ha - ri -

στοῦ - μεν, Κύ - ρι - ε, καὶ δε - ό - με -
stu - men, Ki - ri - e, ke the - o - me -

θά σου, ὁ Θε - ὸς ἡ - μῶν.
tha su, o The - os i - mon.

Priest: We offer to You these gifts
from Your own gifts
in all and for all.

People:

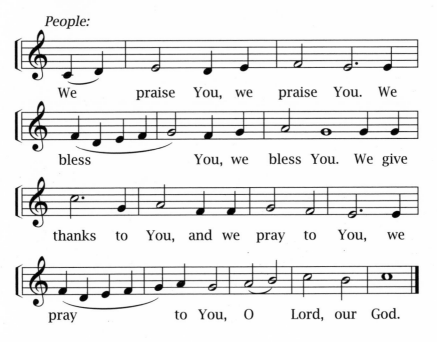

We praise You, we praise You. We
bless You, we bless You. We give
thanks to You, and we pray to You, we
pray to You, O Lord, our God.

67

Ἱερεύς (χαμηλοφώνως): Ὥστε γενέσθαι τοῖς μεταλαμβάνουσιν εἰς νῆψιν ψυχῆς, εἰς ἄφεσιν ἁμαρτιῶν, εἰς κοινωνίαν τοῦ Ἁγίου σου Πνεύματος, εἰς βασιλείας οὐρανῶν πλήρωμα, εἰς παρρησίαν τὴν πρὸς σέ, μὴ εἰς κρῖμα ἢ εἰς κατάκριμα. Ἔτι προσφέρομέν σοι τὴν λογικὴν ταύτην λατρείαν, ὑπὲρ τῶν ἐν πίστει ἀναπαυσαμένων Προπατόρων, Πατέρων, Πατριαρχῶν, Προφητῶν, Ἀποστόλων, Κηρύκων, Εὐαγγελιστῶν, Μαρτύρων, Ὁμολογητῶν, Ἐγκρατευτῶν καὶ παντὸς πνεύματος δικαίου ἐν πίστει τετελειωμένου.

Ἱερεύς· Ἐξαιρέτως τῆς παναγίας, ἀχράντου, ὑπερευλογημένης, ἐνδόξου δεσποίνης ἡμῶν Θεοτόκου καὶ ἀειπαρθένου Μαρίας.

Λαός·

68

Priest: Especially for our most holy, pure, blessed and glorious Lady, the Theotokos and ever virgin Mary.
People:

It is tru - ly   right to call you   bless -

ed, O   The - o - to   -   kos,

ev - er   bless - ed, most   pure and the

moth - er, the moth - er of   our   God.   More

hon   -   'ra - ble   than the   cher - u -

*During the Paschal season, at the Liturgy of St. Basil,
and on great feasts, we sing the designated megalynarion
instead of the above. See pages 298-315.*

Τὴν τι-μι-ω-τέ - ραν τῶν χε-ρου-βεὶμ
Tin ti-mi-o-te - ran ton he-ru-vim

καὶ ἐν-δο-ξο-τέ - ραν ἀ-συγ-
ke en-tho-xo-te - ran a-sin-

κρί - τως τῶν σε-ρα-φείμ,
kri - tos ton se-ra-fim,

τὴν ἀ-δι-αφ-θό - ρως Θε-ὸν
tin a-thi-af-tho - ros The-on

Λό - γον τε-κοῦ - σαν, τὴν
Lo - gon te-ku - san, tin

ὄν-τος Θε-ο-τό - κον, σὲ
on-dos The-o-to - kon, se

με-γα-λύ-νο-μεν.
me-ga-li-no-men.

bim,   and more   glo - rious   be -

yond   com - pare   than   the   ser - a -

phim.   In   vir - gin - i - ty   you   gave

birth   to   God,   to   God   the

Word.   Tru - ly   the   The - o - to -

kos,   we   mag - ni - fy   you,   we

mag - ni - fy   you.

Ἱερεύς (χαμηλοφώνως): Τοῦ ἁγίου Ἰωάννου, προφήτου, προδρόμου καὶ βαπτιστοῦ· τῶν ἁγίων ἐνδόξων καὶ πανευφήμων Ἀποστόλων· τοῦ ἁγίου (Ὄνομα) οὗ καὶ τὴν μνήμην ἐπιτελοῦμεν, καὶ πάντων σου τῶν Ἁγίων, ὧν ταῖς ἱκεσίαις ἐπίσκεψαι ἡμᾶς, ὁ Θεός. Καὶ μνήσθητι πάντων τῶν κεκοιμημένων ἐπ᾽ ἐλπίδι ἀναστάσεως, ζωῆς αἰωνίου (καὶ μνημονεύει ἐνταῦθα ὀνομαστὶ ὧν βούλεται τεθνεώτων) καὶ ἀνάπαυσον αὐτούς, ὁ Θεὸς ἡμῶν, ὅπου ἐπισκοπεῖ τὸ φῶς τοῦ προσώπου σου. Ἔτι παρακαλοῦμέν σε· μνήσθητι, Κύριε, πάσης ἐπισκοπῆς ὀρθοδόξων, τῶν ὀρθοτομούντων τὸν λόγον τῆς σῆς ἀληθείας, παντὸς τοῦ πρεσβυτερίου, τῆς ἐν Χριστῷ διακονίας καὶ παντὸς ἱερατικοῦ τάγματος. Ἔτι προσφέρομέν σοι τὴν λογικὴν ταύτην λατρείαν ὑπὲρ τῆς οἰκουμένης· ὑπὲρ τῆς ἁγίας, καθολικῆς καὶ ἀποστολικῆς Ἐκκλησίας· ὑπὲρ τῶν ἐν ἁγνείᾳ καὶ σεμνῇ πολιτείᾳ διαγόντων· καὶ ὑπὲρ τῶν ἀρχόντων ἡμῶν· δὸς αὐτοῖς Κύριε, εἰρηνικὴν τὴν ἐξουσίαν, ἵνα καὶ ἡμεῖς, ἐν τῇ γαλήνῃ αὐτῶν, ἤρεμον καὶ ἡσύχιον βίον διάγωμεν, ἐν πάσῃ εὐσεβείᾳ καὶ σεμνότητι.

Ἱερεύς· Ἐν πρώτοις, μνήσθητι, Κύριε, τοῦ Ἀρχιεπισκόπου ἡμῶν (ὄνομα), καὶ τοῦ Ἐπισκόπου ἡμῶν (ὄνομα), οὓς χάρισαι ταῖς ἁγίαις σου Ἐκκλησίαις ἐν εἰρήνῃ σώους, ἐντίμους, ὑγιεῖς, μακροημερεύοντας καὶ ὀρθοτομοῦντας τὸν λόγον τῆς σῆς ἀληθείας. Καὶ ὧν ἕκαστος κατὰ διάνοιαν ἔχει καὶ πάντων καὶ πασῶν.
Λαός·

Καὶ πάν-των καὶ πα - σῶν.
Ke pan-don ke pa - son.

Ἱερεύς (χαμηλοφώνως): Μνήσθητι, Κύριε, τῆς πόλεως, ἐν ᾗ παροικοῦμεν, καὶ πάσης πόλεως καὶ χώρας καὶ τῶν πίστει οἰκούντων ἐν αὐταῖς. Μνήσθητι, Κύριε, πλεόντων, ὁδοιπορούντων, νοσούντων, καμνόντων, αἰχμαλώτων καὶ τῆς σωτηρίας αὐτῶν. Μνήσθητι, Κύριε, τῶν καρποφορούντων καὶ καλλιεργούντων ἐν ταῖς ἁγίαις σου Ἐκκλησίαις καὶ μεμνημένων τῶν πενήτων καὶ ἐπὶ πάντας ἡμᾶς τὰ ἐλέη σου ἐξαπόστειλον.

Ἱερεύς· Καὶ δὸς ἡμῖν, ἐν ἑνὶ στόματι καὶ μιᾷ καρδίᾳ δοξάζειν καὶ ἀνυμνεῖν τὸ πάντιμον καὶ μεγαλοπρεπὲς ὄνομά σου, τοῦ Πατρὸς καὶ τοῦ Υἱοῦ καὶ τοῦ Ἁγίου Πνεύματος, νῦν καὶ ἀεὶ καὶ εἰς τοὺς αἰῶνας τῶν αἰώνων.
Λαός·

Ἀ - μήν.
A - min.

Priest (in a low voice): For St. John the prophet, forerunner and baptist; for the holy, glorious and most honorable apostles, for Saint*(s) (name-s)* whom we commemorate today; and for all Your saints, through whose supplications, O God, bless us. Remember also all who have fallen asleep in the hope of resurrection unto eternal life. And grant them rest, our God, where the light of Your countenance shines. Again we ask You, Lord, remember all Orthodox bishops who rightly teach the word of Your truth, all presbyters, all deacons in the service of Christ, and every one in holy orders. We also offer to You this spritual worship for the whole world, for the holy, catholic and apostolic Church, and for those living in purity and holiness. And for all those in public service; permit them, Lord, to serve and govern in peace that through the faithful conduct of their duties we may live peaceful and serene lives in purity and holiness.

Priest: Above all, remember, Lord, our Archbishop *(name)* and our Bishop *(name)*. Grant that they may serve Your holy churches in peace. Keep them safe, honorable, and healthy for many years, rightly teaching the word of Your truth. Remember also, Lord, those whom each of us calls to mind and all Your people.

People:

And all Your peo - ple.

Priest (in a low voice): Remember, Lord, the city in which we live, every city and country and the faithful who dwell in them. Remember, Lord, the travellers, the sick, the suffering and the captives, granting them protection and salvation. Remember, Lord, those who do charitable work, who serve in Your holy churches, and who care for the poor. And send Your mercy upon us all.

Priest: And grant that with one voice and one heart we may glorify and praise Your most honored and majestic name, of the Father + and the Son and the Holy Spirit, now and ever and to the ages of ages.

People:

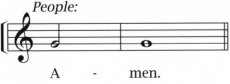

A - men.

73

Ἱερεύς· Καὶ ἔσται τὰ ἐλέη τοῦ μεγάλου Θεοῦ καὶ
Σωτῆρος ἡμῶν Ἰησου Χριστοῦ, μετὰ πάντων ἡμῶν.
Λαός·

Καὶ με - τὰ τοῦ πνεύ-μα - τός   σου.
Ke me-ta tu pnev-ma - tos   su.

Ἱερεύς· Πάντων τῶν ἁγίων μνημονεύσαντες,
ἔτι καὶ ἔτι ἐν εἰρήνῃ τοῦ Κυρίου δεηθῶμεν.
Λαός·

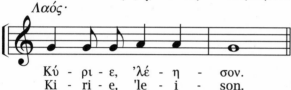

Κύ - ρι - ε, Ἀλέ - η - σον.
Ki - ri - e, 'le - i - son.

Ἱερεύς· Ὑπὲρ τῶν προσκομισθέντων καὶ
ἁγιασθέντων τιμίων δώρων, τοῦ Κυρίου δεηθῶμεν.
Λαός·

Κύ - ρι - ε,   ἐ - λέ - η - σον.
Ki - ri - e,   e - le - i - son.

Ἱερεύς· Ὅπως ὁ φιλάνθρωπος Θεὸς ἡμῶν, ὁ προσδεξάμενος
αὐτὰ εἰς τὸ ἅγιον καὶ ὑπερουράνιον καὶ νοερὸν αὐτοῦ θυσια-
στήριον, εἰς ὀσμὴν εὐωδίας πνευματικῆς, ἀντικαταπέμψῃ ἡμῖν
τὴν θείαν χάριν καὶ τὴν δωρεὰν τοῦ Ἁγίου Πνεύματος, δεηθῶμεν.
Λαός·

Κύ - ρι - ε,   ἐ - λέ - η - σον.
Ki - ri - e,   e - le - i - son.

74

Priest: The mercy of our great God and
Savior Jesus Christ be with all of you.
People:

And with your   spi - rit.

Priest: Having remembered all the saints,
let us again in peace pray to the Lord.
People:

Lord, have mer - cy.

Priest: For the precious Gifts offered and consecrated,
let us pray to the Lord.
People:

Lord,   have mer - cy.

Priest: That our loving God who has received them
at His holy, heavenly and spiritual altar as an offering of
spiritual fragrance, may in return send upon us divine
grace and the gift of the Holy Spirit, let us pray.
People:

Lord,   have mer - cy.

Ἱερεύς· Τὴν ἑνότητα τῆς πίστεως καὶ τὴν κοινωνίαν τοῦ Ἁγίου Πνεύματος αἰτησάμενοι, ἑαυτοὺς καὶ ἀλλήλους καὶ πᾶσαν τὴν ζωὴν ἡμῶν Χριστῷ τῷ Θεῷ παραθώμεθα.

Λαός·

Σόι,   Κύ - ρι - ε.
Si,   Ki - ri - e.

Ἱερεύς (χαμηλοφώνως): Σοὶ παρακατιθέμεθα τὴν ζωὴν ἡμῶν ἅπασαν, καὶ τὴν ἐλπίδα, Δέσποτα φιλάνθρωπε, καὶ παρακαλοῦμέν σε, καὶ δεόμεθα καὶ ἱκετεύομεν. Καταξίωσον ἡμᾶς μεταλαβεῖν τῶν ἐπουρανίων σου καὶ φρικτῶν Μυστηρίων ταύτης τῆς ἱερᾶς καὶ πνευματικῆς Τραπέζης, μετὰ καθαροῦ συνειδότος, εἰς ἄφεσιν ἁμαρτιῶν, εἰς συγχώρησιν πλημμελημά-των, εἰς Πνεύματος Ἁγίου κοινωνίαν, εἰς βασιλείας οὐρανῶν κληρονομίαν, εἰς παρρησίαν τὴν πρὸς σέ, μὴ εἰς κρῖμα, ἢ εἰς κατάκριμα.

ΚΥΡΙΑΚΗ ΠΡΟΣΕΥΧΗ

Ἱερεύς· Καὶ καταξίωσον ἡμᾶς, Δέσποτα, μετὰ παρρησίας, ἀκατακρίτως, τολμᾶν ἐπικαλεῖσθαι σὲ τὸν ἐπουράνιον Θεόν, Πατέρα, καὶ λέγειν·

Ἱερεύς καὶ Λαός·

**Πάτερ ἡμῶν, ὁ ἐν τοῖς οὐρανοῖς·
ἁγιασθήτω τὸ ὄνομά σου·
ἐλθέτω ἡ βασιλεία σου,
γενηθήτω τὸ θέλημά σου,
ὡς ἐν οὐρανῷ καὶ ἐπὶ τῆς γῆς.
Τὸν ἄρτον ἡμῶν τὸν ἐπιούσιον
δὸς ἡμῖν σήμερον·
καὶ ἄφες ἡμῖν τὰ ὀφειλήματα ἡμῶν,
ὡς καὶ ἡμεῖς ἀφίεμεν
τοῖς ὀφειλέταις ἡμῶν·
καὶ μὴ εἰσενέγκῃς ἡμᾶς
εἰς πειρασμόν,
ἀλλὰ ῥῦσαι ἡμᾶς ἀπὸ τοῦ πονηροῦ.**

Priest: Having prayed for the unity of the faith
and the communion of the Holy Spirit,
let us commit ourselves, and one another,
and our whole life to Christ our God.
People:

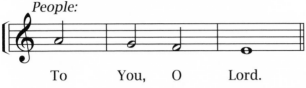

To   You,   O   Lord.

Priest (in a low voice): We entrust to You, Loving Master, our
whole life and hope, and we ask, pray and entreat: make us
worthy to partake of Your heavenly and awesome Mysteries
from this holy and spiritual Table with a clear conscience; for
the remission of sins, forgiveness of transgressions, communion
of the Holy Spirit, inheritance of the kingdom of heaven, confidence before You, and not in judgement or condemnation.

THE LORD'S PRAYER

Priest: And make us worthy, Master, with confidence
and without fear of condemnation, to dare call You,
the heavenly God, FATHER, and to say:

Priest and People:
**Our Father
who art in heaven,
hallowed be thy name.
Thy kingdom come.
Thy will be done on earth
as it is in heaven.
Give us this day our daily bread;
and forgive us our trespasses
as we forgive those
who trespass against us;
and lead us not into temptation,
but deliver us from evil.**

Ἱερεύς· Ὅτι σοῦ ἐστιν ἡ βασιλεία καὶ ἡ δύναμις καὶ ἡ δόξα, τοῦ Πατρὸς καὶ τοῦ Υἱοῦ καὶ τοῦ Ἁγίου Πνεύματος, νῦν καὶ ἀεὶ καὶ εἰς τοὺς αἰῶνας τῶν αἰώνων.
Λαός·

Ἀ - μήν.
A - min.

Ἱερεύς· Εἰρήνη πᾶσι.
Λαός·

Καὶ τῷ πνεύ - μα - τί σου.
Ke to pnev - ma - ti su.

Ἱερεύς· Τὰς κεφαλὰς ἡμῶν τῷ Κυρίῳ κλίνωμεν.
Λαός·

Σόι, Κύ - ρι - ε.
Si, Ki - ri - e.

Ἱερεύς (χαμηλοφώνως): Εὐχαριστοῦμέν σοι, Βασιλεῦ ἀόρατε, ὁ τῇ ἀμετρήτῳ σου δυνάμει τὰ πάντα δημιουργήσας καὶ τῷ πλήθει τοῦ ἐλέους σου ἐξ οὐκ ὄντων εἰς τὸ εἶναι τὰ πάντα παραγαγών. Αὐτὸς Δέσποτα, οὐρανόθεν ἔπιδε ἐπὶ τοὺς ὑποκεκλικότας σοι τὰς ἑαυτῶν κεφαλάς. Οὐ γὰρ ἔκλιναν σαρκὶ καὶ αἵματι, ἀλλὰ σοί, τῷ φοβερῷ Θεῷ. Σὺ οὖν, Δέσποτα, τὰ προκείμενα πᾶσιν ἡμῖν εἰς ἀγαθὸν ἐξομάλισον, κατὰ τὴν ἑκάστου ἰδίαν χρείαν· τοῖς πλέουσι σύμπλευσον· τοῖς ὁδοιποροῦσι συνόδευσον· τοὺς νοσοῦντας ἴασαι, ὁ ἰατρὸς τῶν ψυχῶν καὶ τῶν σωμάτων ἡμῶν.

Ἱερεύς· Χάριτι καὶ οἰκτιρμοῖς καὶ φιλανθρωπίᾳ τοῦ μονογενοῦς σου Υἱοῦ, μεθ' οὗ εὐλογητὸς εἶ, σὺν τῷ παναγίῳ καὶ ἀγαθῷ καὶ ζωοποιῷ σου Πνεύματι, νῦν καὶ ἀεὶ καὶ εἰς τοὺς αἰῶνας τῶν αἰώνων.
Λαός·

Ἀ - μήν.
A - min.

78

Priest: For Yours is the kingdom and the power and the glory,
of the + Father and the Son and the Holy Spirit,
now and ever and to the ages of ages.
People:

A - men.

Priest: Peace be with all.
People:

And with your   spir - it.

Priest: Let us bow our heads to the Lord.
People:

To   You,   O   Lord.

Priest (in a low voice): We give thanks to You, invisible King. By Your
infinite power You created all things and by Your great mercy You
brought everything from nothing into being. Master, look down from
heaven upon those who have bowed their heads before You; they have
bowed not before flesh and blood but before You the awesome God.
Therefore, Master, guide the course of our life for our benefit according to the need of each of us. Travel with those who travel by land, sea
or air; and heal the sick, Physician of our souls and bodies.

Priest: By the grace, mercy, and love for us of Your
only begotten Son, with whom You are blessed
together with Your all holy, good, and life giving Spirit,
now and ever and to the ages of ages.
People:

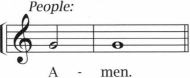

A - men.

Ἱερεύς· Πρόσχωμεν.
Τὰ ἅγια τοῖς ἁγίος.
Λαός·

Εἰς   ἅ - γι - ος,   εἷς   Κύ - ρι - ος,
Is   a - yi - os,   is   Ki - ri - os,

Ἰ - η - σοῦς   Χρι - στός,   εἰς   δό -
I - i - sus   Hri - stos,   is   tho -

ξαν   Θε - οῦ   Πα - τρός.   Ἀ - μήν.
xan   The - u   Pa - tros.   A - min.

Αἱ προσευχαὶ τῆς θείας Κοινωνίας λέγονται χαμηλοφώνως ἀπὸ ὅσους θὰ μεταλάβουν.

Πιστεύω, Κύριε, καὶ ὁμολογῶ ὅτι σὺ εἶ ἀληθῶς ὁ Χριστός, ὁ Υἱὸς τοῦ Θεοῦ τοῦ ζῶντος, ὁ ἐλθὼν εἰς τὸν κόσμον ἁμαρτωλοὺς σῶσαι, ὧν πρῶτός εἰμι ἐγώ. Ἔτι πιστεύω ὅτι τοῦτο αὐτό ἐστι τὸ ἄχραντον Σῶμά σου καὶ τοῦτο αὐτό ἐστι τὸ τίμιον Αἷμά σου. Δέομαι οὖν σου· ἐλέησόν με καὶ συγχώρησόν μοι τὰ παραπτώματά μου, τὰ ἑκούσια καὶ τὰ ἀκούσια, τὰ ἐν λόγῳ, τὰ ἐν ἔργῳ, τὰ ἐν γνώσει καὶ ἐν ἀγνοίᾳ· καὶ ἀξίωσόν με ἀκατακρίτως μετασχεῖν τῶν ἀχράντων σου Μυστηρίων, εἰς ἄφεσιν ἁμαρτιῶν καὶ εἰς ζωὴν αἰώνιον. Ἀμήν.

Ἐν ταῖς λαμπρότησι τῶν ἁγίων σου, πῶς εἰσελεύσομαι ὁ ἀνάξιος; Ἐὰν γὰρ τολμήσω συνεισελθεῖν εἰς τὸν νυμφῶνα, ὁ χιτὼν μὲ ἐλέγχει ὅτι οὐκ ἔστι τοῦ γάμου, καὶ δέσμιος ἐκβαλοῦμαι ὑπὸ τῶν Ἀγγέλων· καθάρισον, Κύριε, τὸν ῥύπον τῆς ψυχῆς μου, καὶ σῶσόν με, ὡς φιλάνθρωπος.

Δέσποτα φιλάνθρωπε, Κύριε Ἰησοῦ Χριστέ, ὁ Θεός μου, μὴ εἰς κρῖμά μοι γένοιτο τὰ ἅγια ταῦτα διὰ τὸ ἀνάξιον εἶναί με, ἀλλ᾽ εἰς κάθαρσιν καὶ ἁγιασμὸν ψυχῆς τε καὶ σώματος καὶ εἰς ἀρραβῶνα μελλούσης ζωῆς καὶ βασιλείας. Ἐμοὶ δὲ τὸ προσκολλᾶσθαι τῷ Θεῷ ἀγαθόν ἐστι, τίθεσθαι ἐν τῷ Κυρίῳ τὴν ἐλπίδα τῆς σωτηρίας μου.

Priest: Let us be attentive.
The holy Gifts for the holy people of God.
People:

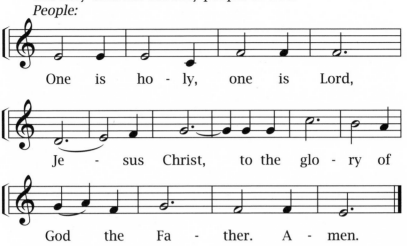

One is ho - ly, one is Lord, Je - sus Christ, to the glo - ry of God the Fa - ther. A - men.

The Communion prayers are recited silently by those prepared to receive the holy Mysteries.

I believe and confess, Lord that You are truly the Christ, the Son of the living God, who came into the world to save sinners, of whom I am the first. I also believe that this is truly Your pure Body and that this is truly Your precious Blood. Therefore, I pray to You, have mercy upon me, and forgive my transgressions, voluntary and involuntary, in word and deed, known and unknown. And make me worthy without condemnation to partake of Your pure Mysteries for the forgiveness of sins and for life eternal. Amen.

How shall I, who am unworthy, enter into the splendor of Your saints? If I dare to enter into the bridal chamber, my clothing will accuse me, since it is not a wedding garment; and being bound up, I shall be cast out by the angels.
In Your love, Lord, cleanse my soul and save me.

Loving Master, Lord Jesus Christ, my God, let not these holy Gifts be to my condemnation because of my unworthiness, but for the cleansing and sanctification of soul and body, and the pledge of the future life and kingdom. It is good for me to cling to God and to place in Him the hope of my salvation.

81

Τοῦ Δείπνου σου τοῦ μυστικοῦ, σήμερον, Υἱὲ Θεοῦ, κοινωνόν με παράλαβε· οὐ μὴ γὰρ τοῖς ἐχθροῖς σου τὸ μυστήριον εἴπω· οὐ φίλημά σοι δώσω καθάπερ ὁ Ἰούδας· ἀλλ᾿ ὡς ὁ ληστὴς ὁμολογῶ σοι· Μνήσθητί μου, Κύριε, ἐν τῇ βασιλείᾳ σου.

Ἰδοὺ προσέρχομαι Χριστῷ τῷ ἀθανάτῳ βασιλεῖ καὶ Θεῷ ἡμῶν.

Η ΘΕΙΑ ΜΕΤΑΛΗΨΙΣ

Τὸ Κοινωνικὸν ἀλλάσει κατὰ τὰς διαφόρους ἑορτάς.

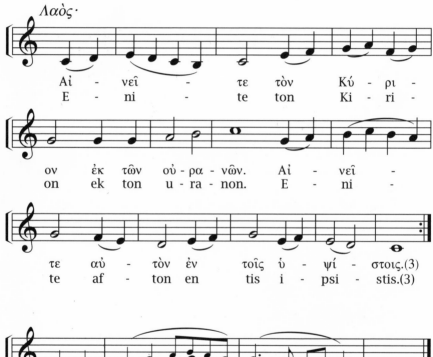

Λαὸς·

Αἰ - νεῖ - τε τὸν Κύ - ρι -
E - ni - te ton Ki - ri -

ον ἐκ τῶν οὐ - ρα - νῶν. Αἰ - νεῖ -
on ek ton u - ra - non. E - ni -

τε αὐ - τὸν ἐν τοῖς ὑ - ψί - στοις.(3)
te af - ton en tis i - psi - stis.(3)

Ἀλ - λη - λού - ϊ - α.
Al - li - lu - i - a.

Ἱερεύς· Μετὰ φόβου Θεοῦ, πίστεως καὶ ἀγάπης προσέλθετε.

Receive me today, O Son of God, as a partaker of Your mystical supper; for I will not betray Your mysteries to Your enemies, nor give You a kiss as did Judas, but as the thief I confess You: Remember me, O Lord, in Your kingdom.

Approaching to receive, each makes a reverence and says:
+ Behold I approach Christ, our immortal King and God.

HOLY COMMUNION

On feast days, during the Paschal season and on weekdays, we sing the designated communion hymn instead of the following. See pages 316-330.

People:

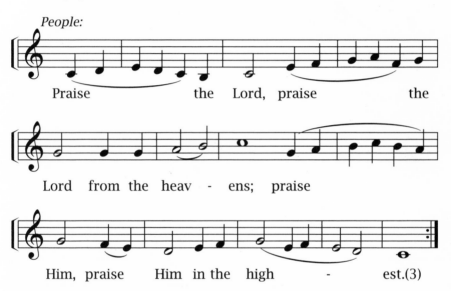

Praise the Lord, praise the Lord from the heav - ens; praise Him, praise Him in the high - est.(3)

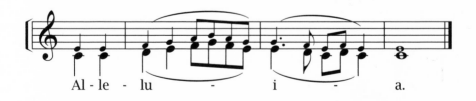

Al - le - lu - i - a.

Priest: Approach with the fear of God, faith and love.

84

Re - ceive me to - day, O Son of

God, as a par - ta - ker of Your

mys - tic - al sup - per; for I will

not be - tray, I will not be - tray Your

mys - t'ries to Your en - e - mies,

nor give You a kiss as did

Ju - das, but as the thief

I con - fess You: Re - mem-ber me, O

85

σοι· Μνή - σθη - τί μου, Κύ - ρι - ε, ὅ - ταν
si: Mni - sthi - ti mu, Ki - ri - e, o - tan

ἔλ - θῃς ἐν τῇ βα - σι - λεί -
el - this en ti va - si - li -

α σου.
a su.

Ἱερεύς· Σῶσον ὁ Θεός τὸν λαόν σου
καὶ εὐλόγησον τὴν κληρονομίαν σου.
Λαός·

Εἴ - δο - μεν τὸ φῶς τὸ ἀ - λη - θι - νόν, ἐ - λά - βο - μεν
I - tho-men to fos to a - li - thi-non, e - la - vo-men

Πνεῦ-μα ἐ-που - ρά - νι - ον, εὕ - ρο - μεν πί-στιν ἀ-λη-
Pnev-ma e-pu - ra - ni - on, ev - ro-men pi-stin a-li-

θῆ, ἀ - δι - αί - ρε-τον Τρι - ά - δα προ-σκυ - νοῦν -
thi, a - thi - e - re-ton Tri - a - tha pro - ski - nun -

τες· αὕ - τη γὰρ ἡ - μᾶς ἔ - σω - σεν.
des; af - ti gar i - mas e - so - sen.

86

Lord, re - mem - ber me, O Lord, in Your

king - dom.

After Communion has been distributed:
Priest: Save, O God, Your people, and + bless Your inheritance.

During the Paschal season we sing Χριστὸς ἀνέστη/Christ is risen
(page 152/153) instead of the following. On great feasts we sing
the apolitikion of the feast. Otherwise we sing:

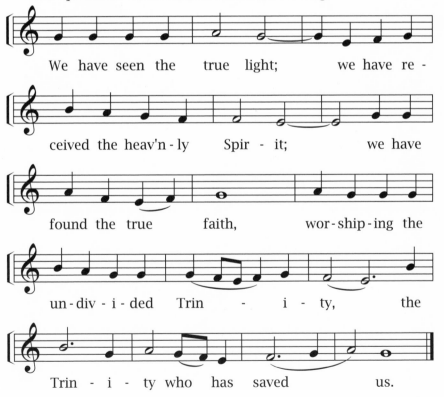

We have seen the true light; we have re -

ceived the heav'n - ly Spir - it; we have

found the true faith, wor - ship - ing the

un - div - i - ded Trin - i - ty, the

Trin - i - ty who has saved us.

Η ΕΥΧΑΡΙΣΤΗΡΙΟΣ ΕΥΧΗ

Ἱερεύς· Ὀρθοί· μεταλαβόντες τῶν θείων, ἁγίων, ἀχράντων, ἀθανάτων, ἐπουρανίων καὶ ζωοποιῶν, φρικτῶν τοῦ Χριστοῦ Μυστηρίων, ἀξίως εὐχαριστήσωμεν τῷ Κυρίῳ.

Λαός·

Κύ - ρι - ε, 'λέ - η - σον.
Ki - ri - e, 'le - i - son.

Ἱερεύς· Ἀντιλαβοῦ, σῶσον, ἐλέησον καὶ διαφύλαξον ἡμᾶς, ὁ Θεός, τῇ σῇ χάριτι.

Λαός·

Κύ - ρι - ε,   ἐ - λέ - η - σον.
Ki - ri - e,   e - le - i - son.

Ἱερεύς· Τὴν ἡμέραν πᾶσαν, τελείαν, ἁγίαν, εἰρηνικὴν καὶ ἀναμάρτητον αἰτησάμενοι, ἑαυτοὺς καὶ ἀλλήλους καὶ πᾶσαν τὴν ζωὴν ἡμῶν Χριστῷ τῷ Θεῷ παραθώμεθα.

Λαός·

Σοί,   Κύ - ρι - ε.
Si,   Ki - ri - e.

Ἱερεύς· Ὅτι σὺ εἶ ὁ ἁγιασμὸς ἡμῶν, καὶ σοὶ τὴν δόξαν ἀναπέμπομεν, τῷ Πατρὶ καὶ τῷ Υἱῷ καὶ τῷ Ἁγίῳ Πνεύματι, νῦν καὶ ἀεὶ καὶ εἰς τοὺς αἰῶνας τῶν αἰώνων.

Λαός·

Ἀ - μήν.
A - min.

THE PRAYER OF THANKSGIVING

Priest: Let us be attentive. Having partaken of the divine, holy, pure, immortal, heavenly, life giving and awesome mysteries of Christ, let us worthily give thanks to the Lord.
People:

Lord, have mer - cy.

Priest: Help us, save us, have mercy upon us and protect us, O God, by Your grace.
People:

Lord, have mer - cy.

Priest: Having prayed for a perfect, holy, peaceful and sinless day, let us commit ourselves, and one another, and our whole life to Christ our God.
People:

To You, O Lord.

Priest: For You are our sanctification and to You we give glory, to the + Father and the Son and the Holy Spirit, now and ever and to the ages of ages.
People:

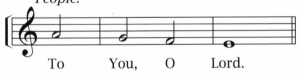

A - men.

ΑΠΟΛΥΣΙΣ

Ἱερεύς·
Ἐν εἰρήνῃ προέλθωμεν. Τοῦ Κυρίου δεηθῶμεν.
Λαός·

Κύ - ρι - ε, ᾽λέ - η - σον.
Ki - ri - e, 'le - i - son.

Ἱερεύς· Ὁ εὐλογῶν τοὺς εὐλογοῦντάς σε, Κύριε, καὶ ἁγιάζων τοὺς ἐπὶ σοὶ πεποιθότας, σῶσον τὸν λαόν σου καὶ εὐλόγησον τὴν κληρονομίαν σου. Τὸ πλήρωμα τῆς Ἐκκλησίας σου φύλαξον, ἁγίασον τοὺς ἀγαπῶντας τὴν εὐπρέπειαν τοῦ οἴκου σου. Σὺ αὐτοὺς ἀντιδόξασον τῇ θεϊκῇ σου δυνάμει καὶ μὴ ἐγκαταλίπῃς ἡμᾶς τοὺς ἐλπίζοντας ἐπὶ σέ. Εἰρήνην τῷ κόσμῳ σου δώρησαι, ταῖς Ἐκκλησίαις σου, τοῖς ἱερεῦσι, τοῖς ἄρχουσι, τῷ στρατῷ καὶ παντὶ τῷ λαῷ σου. Ὅτι πᾶσα δόσις ἀγαθὴ καὶ πᾶν δώρημα τέλειον ἄνωθέν ἐστι καταβαῖνον ἐκ σοῦ τοῦ Πατρὸς τῶν φώτων· καὶ σοὶ τὴν δόξαν καὶ εὐχαριστίαν καὶ προσκύνησιν ἀναπέμπομεν, τῷ Πατρὶ καὶ τῷ Υἱῷ καὶ τῷ Ἁγίῳ Πνεύματι, νῦν καὶ ἀεὶ καὶ εἰς τοὺς αἰῶνας τῶν αἰώνων.
Λαός·

Ἀ - μήν.
A - min.

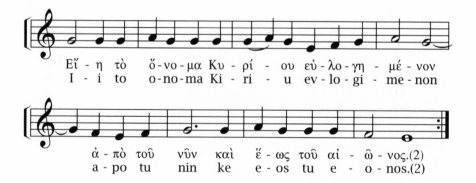

Εἴ - η τὸ ὄ - νο - μα Κυ - ρί - ου εὐ - λο - γη - μέ - νον
I - i to o - no - ma Ki - ri - u ev - lo - gi - me - non

ἀ - πὸ τοῦ νῦν καὶ ἕ - ως τοῦ αἰ - ῶ - νος.(2)
a - po tu nin ke e - os tu e - o - nos.(2)

90

THE DISMISSAL

Priest: Let us depart in peace. Let us pray to the Lord.
People:

Lord, have mer - cy.

Priest: Lord, bless those who praise You and sanctify
those who trust in You. Save Your people and bless Your
inheritance. Protect the whole body of Your Church. Sanctify
those who love the beauty of Your house. Glorify them in
return by Your divine power, and do not forsake those who
hope in You. Grant peace to Your world, to Your Churches,
to the clergy, to those in public service, to the armed forces,
and to all Your people. For every good and perfect gift is from
above, coming from You, the Father of lights. To You we give
glory, thanksgiving and worship, to the + Father and the Son
and the Holy Spirit, now and ever and to the ages of ages.
People:

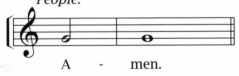

A - men.

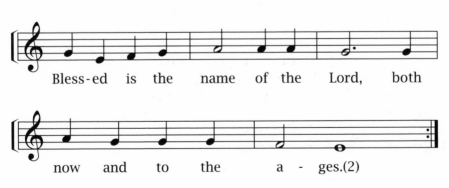

Bless-ed is the name of the Lord, both

now and to the a - ges.(2)

This hymn is continued
on pages 92/93.

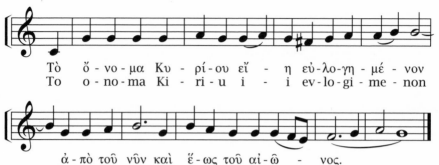

Τὸ ὄ-νο-μα Κυ - ρί-ου εἴ - η εὐ-λο-γη - μέ - νον
To o - no-ma Ki - ri-u i - i ev-lo-gi - me - non

ἀ - πὸ τοῦ νῦν καὶ ἔ - ως τοῦ αἰ - ῶ - νος.
a - po tu nin ke e - os tu e - o - nos.

Ἰερεύς· Τοῦ Κυρίου δεηθῶμεν.
Λαός·

Κύριε, ἐλέησον. Κύριε, ἐλέησον. Κύριε, ἐλέη- σον.
Kirie, eleison. Kirie, eleison. Kirie, elei- son.

Πά - τερ ἅ - γι - ε, εὐ - λό - γη-σον.
Pa - ter a - gi - e, ev - lo - gi-son.
(Δέσποτα) *
(Thespota)

* Ὅταν χοροστατεῖ ἢ
λειτουργεῖ ἐπίσκοπος

Ἰερεύς· Εὐλογία Κυρίου καί ἔλεος ἔλθοι ἐφ' ὑμᾶς,
τῇ αὐτοῦ θεία χάριτι καὶ φιλανθρωπία, πάντοτε,
νῦν καὶ ἀεὶ καὶ εἰς τοὺς αἰῶνας τῶν αἰώνων.
Λαός·

Ἀ - μήν.
A - min.

Bless - ed is the name of the Lord, both

now and to the a - ges.

Priest: Let us pray to the Lord.
People:

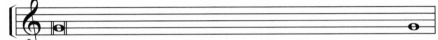

Lord, have mercy. Lord, have mercy. Lord, have mer - cy.

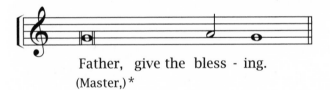

Father, give the bless - ing.
(Master,)*

* Sung when a bishop
is serving the liturgy

Priest: May the blessing of the Lord and His mercy
come upon you through His divine grace and love,
always, now and ever and to the ages of ages.
People:

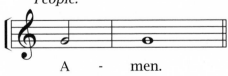

A - men.

93

Ἱερεύς· Δόξα σοι ὁ Θεός, ἡ ἐλπὶς ἡμῶν, δόξα σοι.

Ἱερεύς· [Ὁ ἀνασὰς ἐκ νεκρῶν] Χριστὸς ὁ ἀληθινὸς Θεὸς ἡμῶν...
Λαός·

Τὸν εὐ-λο-γοῦν — τα καὶ ἁ-γι-ά-ζον-τα ἡ - μᾶς,
Ton ev-lo-gun — da ke a-gi-a-zon-da i - mas,

Κύ-ρι-ε φύ-λατ-τε, εἰς πολ-λὰ ἔ - τη.
Ki-ri-e-fi-lat-te, is pol-la e - ti.

Ἱερεύς· ...ταῖς πρεσβείαις τῆς παναχράντου καὶ παναμώμου
ἁγίας αὐτοῦ Μητρός· δυνάμει τοῦ τιμίου καὶ ζωοποιοῦ Σταυροῦ·
προστασίαις τῶν τιμίων ἐπουρανίων Δυνάμεων ἀσωμάτων·
ἱκεσίας τοῦ τιμίου, ἐνδόξου, προφήτου, προδρόμου καὶ βαπτιστοῦ
Ἰωάννου· τῶν ἁγίων, ἐνδόξων καὶ πανευφήμων Ἀποστόλων· τοῦ
ἐν ἁγίοις πατρὸς ἡμῶν Ἰωάννου ἀρχιεπισκόπου Κωνσταντινου-
πόλεως, τοῦ Χρυσοστόμου· τῶν ἁγίων, ἐνδόξων καὶ καλλινίκων
Μαρτύρων· τῶν ἁγίων καὶ ὁσσίων καὶ θεοφόρων Πατέρων ἡμῶν
(τοῦ Ἁγίου τοῦ Ναοῦ), δικαίων θεοπατόρων Ἰωακεὶμ καὶ Ἄννης,
τοῦ Ἁγίου (τῆς ἡμέρας) οὗ καὶ τὴν μνήμην ἐπιτελοῦμεν, καὶ πάντων
τῶν ἁγίων, ἐλεήσαι καὶ σώσαι ἡμᾶς ὡς ἀγαθὸς καὶ φιλάνθρωπος καὶ
ἐλεήμων Θεός.

Δι' εὐχῶν τῶν ἁγίων πατέρων ἡμῶν, Κύριε
Ἰησοῦ Χριστέ, ὁ Θεὸς ἡμῶν, ἐλέησον καὶ σῶσον ἡμᾶς. *
Λαός·

Ἀ - μήν.
A - min.

* Κατὰ τὴν Πασχάλιον περίοδον
λέγεται τὸ Χριστὸς ἀνέστη...

94

Priest: Glory to You, O God, our hope, glory to You.

Priest: May Christ our true God
(on Sundays, he adds: who rose from the dead,*)*
as a good, loving and merciful God,
have mercy on us and save us...

When a bishop is serving, we sing Τὸν δεσπότην, page 343, instead of the hymn below.

People:

Lord, grant long life to him who

bless - es us and sanc-ti - fies us.

Priest:
...through the intercessions of His most pure and holy Mother; the power of the precious and life giving cross; the protection of the honorable, bodiless powers of heaven; the supplications of the honorable, glorious prophet and forerunner, John the Baptist; the holy, glorious and praiseworthy apostles; our father among the saints, John Chrysostom, archbishop of Constantinople; the holy, glorious and triumphant martyrs; our holy and God-bearing fathers *(of the church)*; the holy and righteous ancestors of Christ, Joachim and Anna; Saint *(of the day)* whom we commemorate today, and all the saints.

Through the prayers of our holy fathers, + Lord
Jesus Christ, our God, have mercy on us and save us. *
People:

A - men.

* During the Paschal season the priest says instead: Christ is risen...

95

VARIABLE HYMNS FOR THE DIVINE LITURGY

Apolitikia	98
Kontakia	224
Hymns sung instead of the Trisagion	290
Alternate Cherubic Hymn . . .	294
Megalynaria	298
Communion Hymns	316

THE EIGHT SUNDAY
RESURRECTIONAL APOLITIKIA

Resurrectional Apolitikion
Tone 1

Τοῦ λί - θου σφρα - γι - σθέν - τος ὑ -
Tu li - thu sfra - gi - sthen - dos i -

πὸ τῶν Ἰ - ου - δαί - ων καὶ στρα - τι - ω -
po ton I - u - the - on ke stra - ti - o -

τῶν φυ - λασ - σόν - των τὸ ἄ - χραν - τον σου
ton fi - las - son - don to a - hran - don su

σῶ - μα, ἀ - νέ - στης τρι - ή - με - ρος Σω -
so - ma, a - ne - stis tri - i - me - ros So -

τήρ, δω - ρού - με - νος τῷ κό - σμῳ τὴν ζω -
tir, tho - ru - me - nos to ko - smo tin zo -

98

Resurrectional Apolitikion
Tone 1

Τοῦ λίθου σφραγισθέντος

Al - though Your tomb was sealed with a

stone, O Sav - ior, and Your most pure

bo - dy was guard-ed by the sol - diers, You

rose on the third day giv-ing

life to all the world. There - fore, O

99

ήν. Δι - ὰ   τοῦ - το αἱ δυ - νά - μεις τῶν οὐ-ρα-
in. Thi - a   tu - to e thi - na - mis ton u -ra-

νῶν   ἐ - βό - ων σοι, ζω-ο - δό - τα·
non   e - vo - on si, zo-o - tho - ta:

Δό - ξα τῇ ἀ - να - στά-σει σου Χρι - στέ,
Tho - xa ti a - na - sta-si su Hri - ste,

δό - ξα τῇ βα - σι - λεί - ᾳ σου,
tho - xa ti va - si - li - a su,

δό - ξα τῇ οἰ - κο - νο - μί - ᾳ σου,
tho - xa ti i - ko - no - mi - a su,

μό - νε φι - λάν - θρω - - πε.
mo - ne fi - lan - thro - - pe.

giv - er of life, the pow - ers of heav - en

praise You: Glo - ry to Your res - ur -

rec - tion, O Christ. Glo - ry to Your

king - dom. Glo - ry to Your sav - ing wis - dom, O

on - ly lov - er of man - kind.

Resurrectional Apolitikion
Tone 2

Ὅ - τε κα - τῆλ - θες πρὸς τὸν
O - te ka - til - thes pros ton

θά - να - τον ἡ ζω - ἡ ἡ ἀ -
tha - na - ton i zo - i i a -

θά - να - τος, τό - τε τὸν
tha - na - tos, to - te ton

Ἅ - δην ἐ - νέ - κρω - σας,
A - thin e - ne - kro - sas,

τῇ ἀ - στρα - πῇ - τῆς θε - ό - τη - τος·
ti a - stra - pi tis the - o - ti - tos.

Ὅ - τε δὲ καὶ τοὺς τεθ - νε - ῶ - τας ἐκ τῶν
O - te the ke tus te - thne - o - tas ek ton

102

Resurrectional Apolitikion
Tone 2

Ὅτε κατῆλθες

When You de - scend-ed in - to death, Life im-

mor - tal, You van-quished the pow'r of

hell by your re - splen-dent div - in - i -

ty, and when You raised the dead from the

depths of dark - ness, all the

heav-en - ly pow - ers cried out tri -

κα - τα - χθο - νί - ων ἀ - νέ - στη - σας,
ka - ta - htho - ni - on a - ne - sti - sas,

πᾶ - σαι αἱ δυ - νά - μεις τῶν ἐ - που - ρα -
pa - se e thi - na - mis ton e - pu - ra -

νί - ων ἐ - κραύ - γα - ζον·
ni - on e - krav - ga - zon:

Ζω - ο - δό - τα, Χρι - στὲ ὁ Θε -
Zo - o - tho - ta, Hri - ste o The -

ὸς ἡ - μῶν, δό - ξα σοι.
os i - mon, tho - xa si.

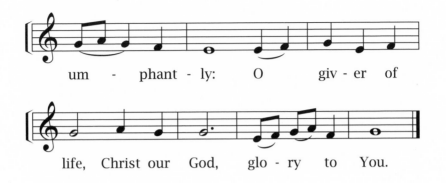

um - phant - ly: O giv - er of life, Christ our God, glo - ry to You.

Resurrectional Apolitikion
Tone 3

Εὐ - φραι - νέ - σθω τὰ οὐ -
Ef - fre - nes - tho ta u -

ρά - νι - α, ἀ - γαλ - λι - ά - σθω τὰ ἐ -
ra - ni - a, a - gal - li - a - stho ta e -

πί - γει - α, ὅ - τι ἐ - ποί - η - σε
pi - yi - a, o - ti e - pi - i - se

κρά - τος, ἐν βρα - χί - ο - νι αὐ - τοῦ ὁ
kra - tos, en vra - hi - o - ni af - tu o

Κύ - ρι - ος. Ἐ - πά - τη - σε τῷ θα -
Ki - ri - os. E - pa - ti - se to tha -

νά - τῳ τὸν θά - να - τον· πρω-
na - to ton tha - na - ton; pro-

106

Resurrectional Apolitikion
Tone 3

Εὐφραινέσθω τὰ οὐράνια

Let the heav - ens re - joice and the

earth be glad, for the

Lord has shown the might - y

pow - er of His arm. He has

tram-pled down death by

death, be - com - ing the first - born

τό - το - κος   τῶν νε - κρῶν ἐ - γέ - νε - το·
to - to - kos   ton ne - kron e - ge - ne - to.

Ἐκ   κοι - λί - ας   ᾅ - δου ἐρ -
Ek   ki - li - as   a - thu er -

ρύ -, σα - το ἡ - μᾶς,   καὶ πα -
ri - sa - to i - mas,   ke pa -

ρέσ - χε τῷ κό - σμῳ τὸ μέ - γα
res - he to ko - smo to me - ga

ἔ - λε - ος.
e - le - os.

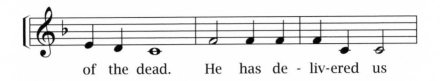

of the dead. He has de - liv-ered us

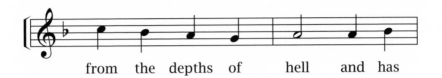

from the depths of hell and has

grant - ed to all the world His great

mer - cy.

Resurrectional Apolitikion
Tone 4

Τὸ φαι - δρὸν τῆς ἀ - να - στά - σε - ως
To fe - thron tis a - na - sta - se - os

κή - ρυγ - μα, ἐκ τοῦ ἀγ - γέ - λου μα -
ki - rig - ma, ek tu an - ge - lu ma -

θοῦ - σαι αἱ τοῦ Κυ - ρί - ου μα -
thu - se e tu Ki - ri - u ma -

θή - τρι - αι, καὶ τὴν προ - γο - νι -
thi - tri - e, ke tin pro - go - ni -

κὴν ἀ - πό - φα - σιν ἀ - πορ - ρί - ψα - σαι,
kin a - po fa - sin a - por - ri - psa - se,

τοῖς ἀ - πο - στό - λοις καυ - χό - με - ναι
tis a - po - sto - lis kaf - ho - me - ne

110

Resurrectional Apolitikion
Tone 4

Τὸ φαιδρὸν

The joy - ful news of Your res - ur -

rec - tion was pro - claimed by the

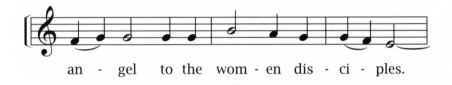

an - gel to the wom - en dis - ci - ples.

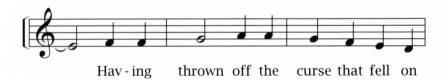

Hav - ing thrown off the curse that fell on

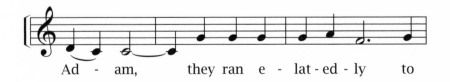

Ad - am, they ran e - lat - ed - ly to

111

ἔ - λε - γον·   Ἐ - σκύ - λευ - ται   ὁ
e - le - gon: E - ski - lef - te   o

θά - να - τος,   ἡ   γέρ - θη   Χρι -
tha - na - tos,   i   ger - thi   Hri -

στὸς   ὁ Θε - ός,   δω - ρού - με - νος   τῷ
stos   o The - os,   tho - ru - me - nos   to

κόσ - μῳ   τὸ μέ - γα   ἔ - λε - ος.
ko - smo   to me - ga   e - le - os.

tell   the   a - pos - tles: Death   has   been

van - quished; Christ our God is   ris - en from the

dead,   bless - ing all the   world with His great

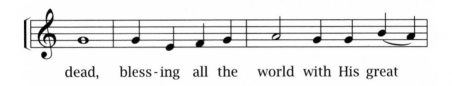

mer -   cy.

Resurrectional Apolitikion
Tone 5

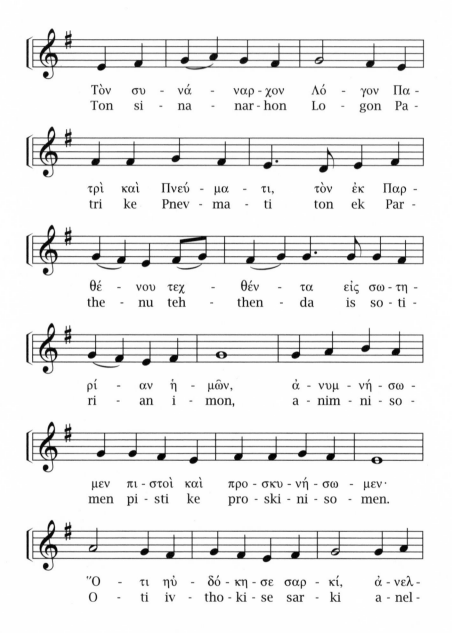

Τὸν συ - νά - ναρ - χον Λό - γον Πα -
Ton si - na - nar - hon Lo - gon Pa -

τρὶ καὶ Πνεύ - μα - τι, τὸν ἐκ Παρ -
tri ke Pnev - ma - ti ton ek Par -

θέ - νου τεχ - θέν - τα εἰς σω - τη -
the - nu teh - then - da is so - ti -

ρί - αν ἡ - μῶν, ἀ - νυμ - νή - σω -
ri - an i - mon, a - nim - ni - so -

μεν πι - στοὶ καὶ προ - σκυ - νή - σω - μεν·
men pi - sti ke pro - ski - ni - so - men.

Ὅ - τι ηὐ - δό - κη - σε σαρ - κί, ἀ - νελ -
O - ti iv - tho - ki - se sar - ki a - nel -

114

Resurrectional Apolitikion
Tone 5

Τὸν συνάναρχον Λόγον

To the Word, co - e - ter - nal with the
Fa - ther and the Spir - it,
born of the Vir - gin for our sal -
va - tion, let us, the
faith - ful, give praise and wor -
ship. For He willed to be lift - ed

θεῖν ἐν τῷ σταυ - ρῷ καὶ
thin en to stav - ro ke

θά - να - τον ὑ - πο - μεῖ - ναι, καὶ ἐ -
tha - na - ton i - po - mi - ne, ke e -

γεῖ - ραι τοὺς τε - θνε - ῶ - τας ἐν τῇ ἐν
gi - re tus te - thne - o - tas, en ti en -

δό - ξῳ ἀ - να - στά - σει αὐ - τοῦ.
tho - xo a - na - sta - si af - tu.

up on the cross in the flesh, to en-
dure death and raise the dead by His
glo-rious res-ur-rec-tion.

Resurrectional Apolitikion
Tone 6

Ἀγ - γε - λι - καὶ δυ - νά - μεις ἐ -
An - ge - li - ke thi - na - mis e -

πὶ τὸ μνῆ - μά σου, καὶ οἱ φυ -
pi to mni - ma su, ke i fi -

λάσ - σον - τες ἀ - πε - νε - κρώ - θη - σαν· καὶ
las - son - des a - pe - ne - kro - thi - san; ke

ἵ - στα - το Μα - ρί - α ἐν τῷ
i - sta - to Ma - ri - a en to

τά - φῳ ζη - τοῦ - σα τὸ
ta - fo zi - tu - sa to

ἄ - χραν - τόν σου σῶ - μα. Ἐ -
a - hran - don su so - ma. E -

118

Resurrectional Apolitikion
Tone 6

Ἀγγελικαὶ δυνάμεις

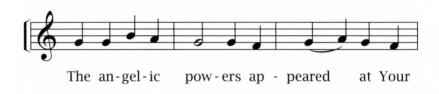

The an-gel-ic   pow-ers ap - peared   at Your

tomb,   the sol-diers   guard-ing it be-came as

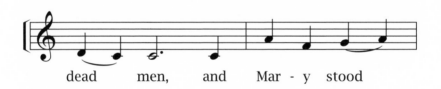

dead   men,   and   Mar - y   stood

at   Your grave   seek   -   ing,

seek - ing Your most pure   bod-y. But

σκύ - λευ - σας τὸν ἄ - δην, μὴ πει - ρασ -
ski - lef - sas ton a - thin, mi pi - ras -

θεὶς ὑπ' αὐ - τοῦ· ὑ -
this ip' af - tu; i -

πήν - τη - σας τῇ Παρ - θέ - νῳ, δο -
pin - di - sas ti Par - the - no, tho -

ρού - με - νος τὴν ζω - ὴν. Ὁ ἀ - να -
ru - me - nos tin zo - in. O a - na -

στὰς ἐκ τῶν νε - κρῶν,
stas ek ton ne - kron,

Κύ - ρι - ε, δό - ξα σοι.
Ki - ri - e, tho - xa si.

You made hell a cap - tive; You were un -

touched by its might. You came to the

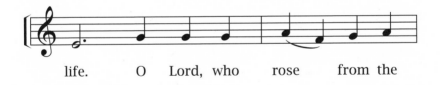

vir - gin and grant - ed

life. O Lord, who rose from the

dead, glo - ry to You.

Resurrectional Apolitikion
Tone 7

Κα - τέ - λυ - σας τῷ σταυ - ρῷ
Ka - te - li - sas to stav - ro

σου τὸν θά - να - τον· ἡ - νέ - ω - ξας
su ton tha - na - ton; i - ne - o - xas

τῷ λη - στῇ τὸν πα - ρά - δει - σον· τῶν
to li - sti ton pa - ra - thi - son; ton

μυ - ρο - φό - ρων τὸν θρῆ - νον με - τέ - βα -
mi - ro - fo - ron ton thri - non me - te - va -

λες καὶ τοῖς σοῖς ἀ - πο - στό - λοις κη -
les ke tis sis a - po - sto - lis ki -

ρύτ - τειν ἐ - πέ - τα - ξας· ὅ - τι ἀ -
rit - tin e - pe - ta - xas, o - ti a -

Resurrectional Apolitikion
Tone 7

Κατέλυσας τῷ σταυρῷ

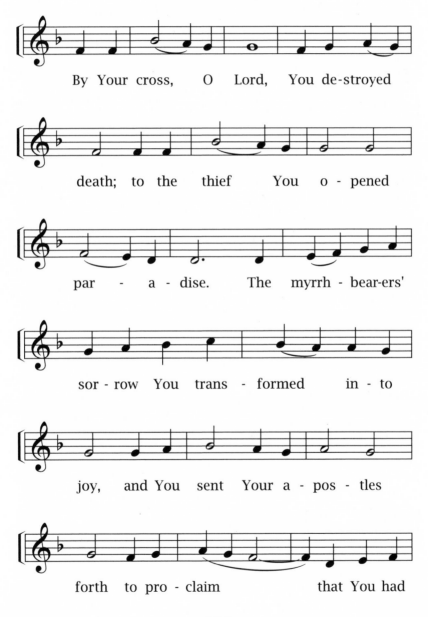

By Your cross, O Lord, You de-stroyed

death; to the thief You o - pened

par - a - dise. The myrrh - bear-ers'

sor - row You trans - formed in - to

joy, and You sent Your a - pos - tles

forth to pro - claim that You had

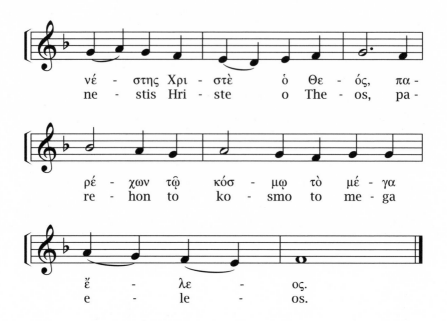

νέ - στης Χρι - στὲ   ὁ Θε - ός,   πα -
ne - stis Hri - ste   o The - os,   pa -

ρέ - χων τῷ   κόσ - μῳ τὸ   μέ - γα
re - hon to   ko - smo to   me - ga

ἔ - λε - ος.
e - le - os.

ris - en from the dead, Christ our God, be -

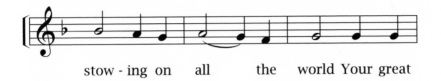

stow - ing on all the world Your great

mer - cy.

Resurrectional Apolitikion
Tone 8

Ἐξ ὕ - ψους κα - τῆλ - θες ὁ
Ex i - psus ka - til - thes o

εὔ - σπλαγ - χνος, τα - φὴν κα - τε -
ev - spla - hnos, ta - fin ka - te -

δέ - ξω τρι - ή - με - ρον,
the - xo tri - i - me - ron,

ἵ - να ἡ - μᾶς ἐ - λευ - θε - ρώ - σῃς τῶν πα -
i - na i - mas e - lef - the - ro - sis ton pa -

θῶν, ἡ ζω - ὴ καὶ ἡ ἀ - νά - στα - σις ἡ -
thon, i zo - i ke i a - na - sta - sis i -

μῶν, Κύ - ρι - ε, δό - ξα σοι.
mon, Ki - ri - e, tho - xa si.

126

Resurrectional Apolitikion
Tone 8

Ἐξ ὕψους κατῆλθες

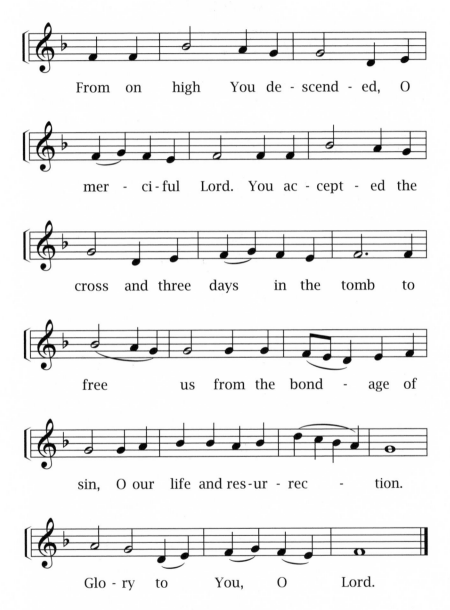

From on high You de - scend - ed, O

mer - ci - ful Lord. You ac - cept - ed the

cross and three days in the tomb to

free us from the bond - age of

sin, O our life and res - ur - rec - tion.

Glo - ry to You, O Lord.

APOLITIKIA FROM THE TRIODION

The First Sunday of Lent — Sunday of Orthodoxy

Apolitikion

Τὴν ἄ - χραν - τον εἰ - κό - να σου προ - σκυ -
Tin a - hran - don i - ko - na sou pro - ski -

νοῦ - μεν Ἀ - γα - θέ, αἰ - τού - με - νοι συγ -
nu - men A - ga - the, e - tu - me - ni siy -

χώ - ρη - σιν τῶν πται - σμά - των ἡ - μῶν, Χρι -
ho - ri - sin ton pte - sma - ton i - mon, Hri -

στὲ ο Θε - ός. Βου - λή - σει γαρ ηὐ -
ste o The - os. Vu - li - si gar iv -

δό - κη - σας σαρ - κὶ ἀ - νελ - θεῖν ἐν τῷ σταυ -
tho - ki - sas sar - ki a - nel - thin en to stav -

ρῷ ἵ - να ρύ - ση οὓς ἔ - πλα - σας
ro i - na ri - si - us e - pla - sas

128

The First Sunday of Lent — Sunday of Orthodoxy
Apolitikion

Τὴν ἄχραντον εἰκόνα σου

Be - fore Your most pure im - age we bow

down, O Good One, en - treat-ing You to for-

give our sins, Christ our God. For You

wil - ling - ly as - cend - ed the cross in the

flesh to de - liv - er from the en - e - my

those whom You had made. For this we

129

ἐκ τῆς δου - λεί - ας τοῦ ἐχ - θροῦ·
ek tis thu - li - as tu eh - thru;

ὅ - θεν εὐ - χα - ρί - στως βο - ῶ - μεν σοι·
o - then ef - ha - ri - stos vo - o - men si:

χα - ρᾶς ἐ - πλή - ρω - σας τὰ πάν - τα ὁ Σω -
ha - ras e - pli - ro - sas ta pan - da o So -

τὴρ ἡ - μῶν· πα - ρα - γε - νό - με -
tir i - mon; pa - ra - ge - no - me -

νος εἰς τὸ σῶ - σαι τὸν κό - σμον.
nos is to so - se ton ko - smon.

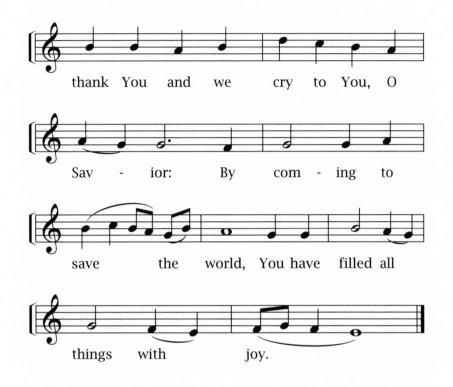

thank You and we cry to You, O

Sav - ior: By com - ing to

save the world, You have filled all

things with joy.

The Second Sunday of Lent — St. Gregory Palamas
Apolitikion

Ὀρ - θο - δο - ξί - ας ὁ φω - στήρ, Ἐκ - κλη -
Or - tho - tho - xi - as o fo - stir, ek - kli -

σί - ας τὸ στή - ριγ - μα καὶ δι - δά - σκα -
si - as to sti - rig - ma ke thi - tha - ska -

λε, τῶν μο - να - στῶν ἡ καλ - λο -
le, ton mo - na - ston i kal - lo -

νή, τῶν θε - ο - λό - γων ὑ -
ni, ton the - o - lo - gon i -

πέρ - μα - χος ἀ - προ - σμά - χη -
per - ma - hos a - pro - sma - hi -

τος, Γρη - γό - ρι - ε θαυ - μα - τουρ -
tos, Gri - go - ri - e thav - ma - tur -

γέ, Θεσ - σα - λο - νί - κης τὸ καύ - χη - μα,
ge, Thes - sa - lo - ni - kis to kaf - hi - ma,

The Second Sunday of Lent — St. Gregory Palamas
Apolitikion

Ὀρθοδοξίας ὁ φωστήρ

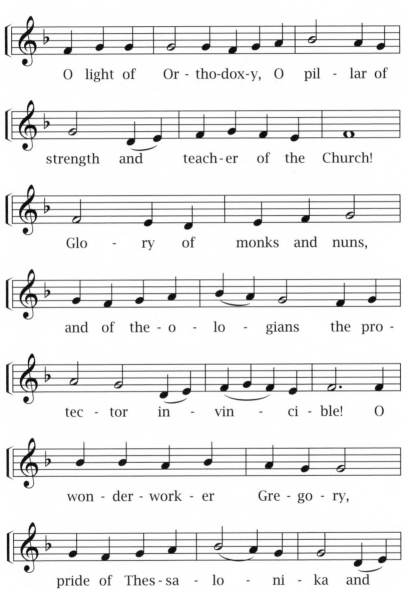

O light of Or - tho-dox-y, O pil - lar of strength and teach-er of the Church! Glo - ry of monks and nuns, and of the - o - lo - gians the pro - tec - tor in - vin - ci - ble! O won - der - work - er Gre - go - ry, pride of Thes - sa - lo - ni - ka and

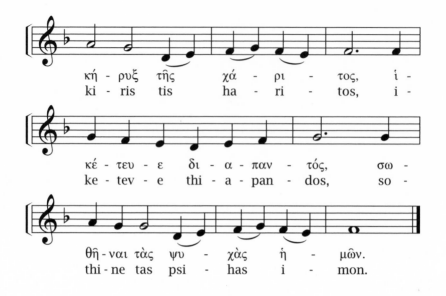

κή - ρυξ τῆς χά - ρι - τος, ἱ -
ki - ris tis ha - ri - tos, i -

κέ - τευ - ε δι - α - παν - τός, σω -
ke - tev - e thi - a - pan - dos, so -

θῆ - ναι τὰς ψυ - χὰς ἡ - μῶν.
thi - ne tas psi - has i - mon.

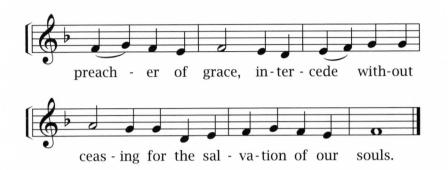

preach - er of grace, in - ter - cede with-out

ceas - ing for the sal - va - tion of our souls.

The Fourth Sunday of Lent — St. John of *The Ladder*
Apolitikion

Ταῖς τῶν δα - κρύ - ων σου ρο - αῖς, τῆς ἐ -
Tes ton tha - kri - on su ro - es, tis e -

ρή - μου τὸ ἄ - γο - νον ἐ - γε -
ri - mu to a - go - non e - ge -

ώρ - γη - σας, καὶ τοῖς ἐκ
or - gi - sas, ke tis ek

βά - θους στε - ναγ - μοῖς, εἰς ἐ - κα - τὸν τοὺς
va - thus ste - nag - mis, is e - ka - ton tus

πό - νους ἐ - καρ - πο - φό - ρη -
po - nus e - kar - po - fo - ri -

σας; καὶ γέ - γο - νας φω -
sas; ke ge - go - nas fo -

στήρ τῇ οἰ - κου - μέ - νη
stir ti i - ku - me - ni

The Fourth Sunday of Lent — St. John of *The Ladder*
Apolitikion

Ταῖς τῶν δακρύων σου

Like warm and gen - tle rain, your

tears of com - punc - tion made the

de - sert burst forth in

bloom. Your pa - tient en -

du - rance made your suf - f'rings bear

fruit one - hun - dred - fold and your

won - drous deeds have filled all the world with

λάμ - πων τοῖς θαύ - μα - σιν, Ἰ - ω -
lam - bon tis thav - ma - sin, I - o -

άν - νη πα - τὴρ ἡ - μῶν
an - ni pa - tir i - mon

ὅ - σι - ε· πρέ - σβευ - ε Χρι -
o - si - e; pre - svev - e Hri -

στῷ τῷ Θε - ῷ σω - θῆ - ναι τὰς ψυ -
sto to The - o so - thi - ne tas psi -

χὰς ἡ - μῶν.
has i - mon.

138

light. O ho - ly fa - ther

John, in - ter - cede with Christ our God to

save our souls.

The Fifth Sunday of Lent—St. Mary of Egypt
Apolitikion

Ἐν σοὶ μῆ-τερ ἀ-κρι-βῶς δι-ε-
En si, mi-ter a-kri-vos thi-e-

σώ-θη τὸ κατ' εἰ-κό - να· λα-βοῦ-σα
so-thi to kat' i-ko - na; la-vu-sa

γὰρ τὸν σταυ-ρόν, ἠ-κο-λού-θη-σας τῷ Χρι-
gar ton stav-ron, i-ko-lu-thi-sas to Hri-

στῷ, καὶ πρά-τ-του-σα ἐ-δί-δα -
sto, ke prat-tu-sa e-thi-tha

σκες, ὑ-πε-ρο-ρᾶν μὲν σαρ-κός, πα-
skes, i-pe-ro-ran men sar-kos, pa-

ρέρ-χε-ται γάρ· ἐ-πι-με-λεῖ-σθαι δὲ ψυ-χῆς,
rer-he-te gar; e-pi-me-li-sthe the psi-his,

πράγ-μα-τος ἀ-θα - νά -
prag-ma-tos a-tha - na -

The Fifth Sunday of Lent—St. Mary of Egypt
Apolitikion

Ἐν σοὶ μῆτερ ἀκριβῶς

In you, ho - ly moth - er Mar - y, the
im - age of God shone forth, for you
took up your cross and fol - lowed the
Lord. By word and ex - am - ple you
taught us to live in the spir - it while
still in the flesh. There - fore your
spir - it re - joic - es with the
an - gels for - ev - er.

141

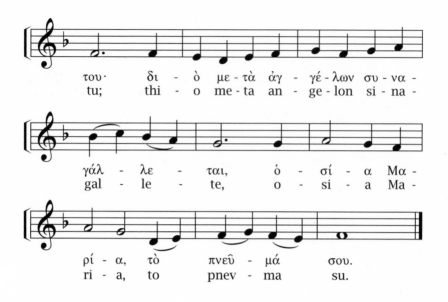

τον·   δι - ὸ με - τὰ ἀγ - γέ - λων συ - να -
tu;   thi - o me - ta an - ge - lon si - na -

γάλ - λε - ται,   ὁ - σί - α Μα -
gal - le - te,   o - si - a Ma -

ρί - α, τὸ   πνεῦ - μά   σου.
ri - a, to   pnev - ma   su.

Lazarus Saturday / Palm Sunday
Apolitikion

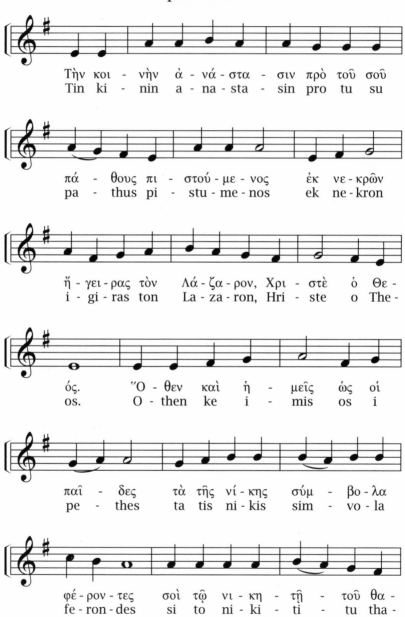

Τὴν κοι - νὴν ἀ - νά - στα - σιν πρὸ τοῦ σοῦ
Tin ki - nin a - na - sta - sin pro tu su

πά - θους πι - στού - με - νος ἐκ νε - κρῶν
pa - thus pi - stu - me - nos ek ne - kron

ἤ - γει - ρας τὸν Λά - ζα - ρον, Χρι - στὲ ὁ Θε -
i - gi - ras ton La - za - ron, Hri - ste o The -

ός. Ὅ - θεν καὶ ἡ - μεῖς ὡς οἱ
os. O - then ke i - mis os i

παῖ - δες τὰ τῆς νί - κης σύμ - βο - λα
pe - thes ta tis ni - kis sim - vo - la

φέ - ρον - τες σοὶ τῷ νι - κη - τῇ - τοῦ θα -
fe - ron - des si to ni - ki - ti - tu tha -

144

Lazarus Saturday / Palm Sunday
Apolitikion

Τὴν κοινὴν ἀνάστασιν

Be - fore Your pas - sion You con -

firmed the res - ur - rec - tion of

all by rais - ing Laz' - rus from the

dead, O Christ our God.

There-fore, like the child-ren of old, we

al - so car - ry sym - bols of vic - to - ry,

νά - του βο - ῶ - μεν· Ὡ - σαν -
na - tu vo - o - men: O - san -

να ἐν τοῖς ὑ - ψί - στοις, εὐ - λο - γη -
na en tis i - psi - stis, ev - lo - gi -

μέ - νος ὁ ἐρ - χό - με - νος ἐν ὁ -
me - nos o er - ho - me - nos en o -

νό - μα - τι Κυ - ρί - ου.
no - ma - ti Ki - ri - u.

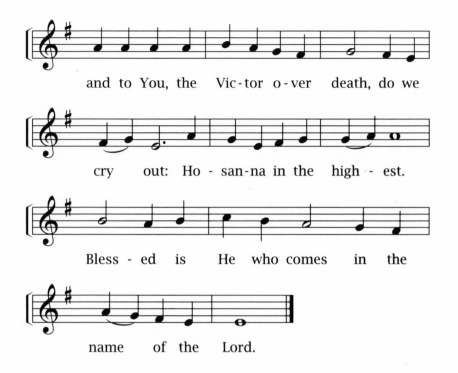

and to You, the Vic-tor o-ver death, do we

cry out: Ho - san-na in the high - est.

Bless - ed is He who comes in the

name of the Lord.

Συν - τα - φέν - τες σοι δι - ὰ τοῦ βα -
Sin - da - fen - des si thi - a tu va -

πτί - σμα - τος, Χρι - στὲ ο Θε - ὸς ἠ -
pti - sma - tos, Hri - ste o The - os i -

μῶν, τῆς ἀ - θα - νά - του ζω -
mon, tis a - tha - na - tu zo -

ῆς ἠ - ξι - ώ - θη - μεν τῇ ἀ - να -
is i - xi - o - thi - men ti a - na -

στά - σει σου, καὶ α - νυ - μνοῦν - τες
sta - si su, ke a - ni - mnun - des

κρά - ζο - μεν· Ὡ - σαν - να ἐν τοῖς ὑ -
kra - zo - men: O - san - na en tis i -

148

Palm Sunday
Another Apolitikion

Συνταφέντες σοι

In our bap - ti - sm we were bur-ied with

You, O Christ our God, and by Your res-ur-

rec-tion you have grant-ed us e - ter - nal life.

There-fore, we sing Your prais - es, O Lord:

Ho-san-na in the high - est. Bless-ed is

He who comes in the name of the Lord.

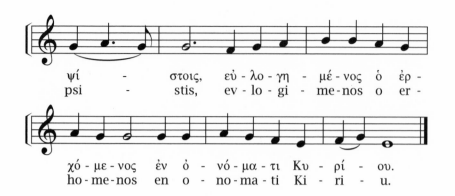

ψί - στοις, εὐ - λο - γη - μέ - νος ὁ ἐρ -
psi - stis, ev - lo - gi - me - nos o er -

χό - με - νος ἐν ὀ - νό - μα - τι Κυ - ρί - ου.
ho - me - nos en o - no - ma - ti Ki - ri - u.

APOLITIKIA FROM THE PENTECOSTARION

Pascha
Apolitikion

Χρι - στὸς ἀ - νέ - στη
Hri - stos a - ne - sti

ἐκ νε - κρῶν, θα - νά - τῳ
ek ne - kron, tha - na - to

θά - να - τον πα - τή -
tha - na - ton pa - ti -

σας, καὶ τοῖς ἐν τοῖς
sas, ke tis en tis

μνή - μα - σι ζω - ὴν χα - ρι -
mni - ma - si zo - in ha - ri -

σά - με - νος.
sa - me - nos.

152

Pascha
Apolitikion

Χριστὸς ἀνέστη

Christ is ri - sen from the dead, tram - pling down death by death and on those in the grave be - stow - ing life.

153

Sunday of Thomas — First Sunday after Pascha
Apolitikion

Ἐ - σφρα - γι - σμέ - νου τοῦ
E - sfra - gi - sme - nu tu

μνή - μα - τος, ἡ ζω - ἡ ἐκ τά - φου ἀ -
mni - ma - tos, i zo - i ek ta - fu a -

νέ - τει - λας, Χρι - στὲ ὁ Θε - ός· καὶ τῶν θυ -
ne - ti - las, Hri - ste o The - os; ke ton thi -

ρῶν κε - κλει - σμέ - νων, τοῖς μα - θη - ταῖς ἐ -
ron ke - kli - sme - non, tis ma - thi - tes e -

πέ - στης ἡ πάν - των ἀ - νά - στα - σις,
pe - stis i pan - don a - na - sta - sis,

Πνεῦ - μα εὐ - θὲς δι' αὐ -
Pnev - ma ef - thes thi' af -

154

Sunday of Thomas — First Sunday after Pascha
Apolitikion

Ἐσφραγισμένου τοῦ μνήματος

While the tomb was sealed You shone

forth from it as light, O our life, Christ our

God. And though the doors were

closed You ap - peared in the midst of Your dis-

ci - ples. O re - sur - rec - tion of

all, through them re - store in us a new

spir - it in Your great

155

τῶν ἐγ - και - νί - ζων ἡ - μῖν, κα - τὰ τὸ
ton en - ge - ni - zon i - min, ka - ta to

μέ - γα σου ἔ - λε -
me - ga su e - le -

ος.
os.

mer - cy.

The Sunday of the Myrrh-bearing Women
Apolitikion

Ὁ εὐ - σχή - μων Ἰ - ω - σὴφ ἀ - πὸ τοῦ
O efs - hi - mon I - o - sif a - po tu

ξύ - λου κα - θε - λὼν τὸ ἄ - χραν - τόν σου
xi - lu ka - the - lon to a - hran - don su

σῶ - μα, σιν -
so - ma, sin -

δό - νι κα - θα - ρᾷ εἰ - λή - σας καὶ ἀ -
tho - ni ka - tha - ra i - li - sas ke a -

ρω - μα - σιν, ἐν μνή - μα - τι και -
ro - ma - sin, en mni - ma - ti ke -

νῷ κι - δεύ - σας ἀ - πε - θε -
no ki - thev - sas a - pe - the -

το· ἀλ - λὰ τρι - ἡ - με - ρος ἀ -
to: al - la tri - i - me - ros a -

The Sunday of the Myrrh-bearing Women
Apolitikion

Ὁ εὐσχήμων Ἰωσὴφ

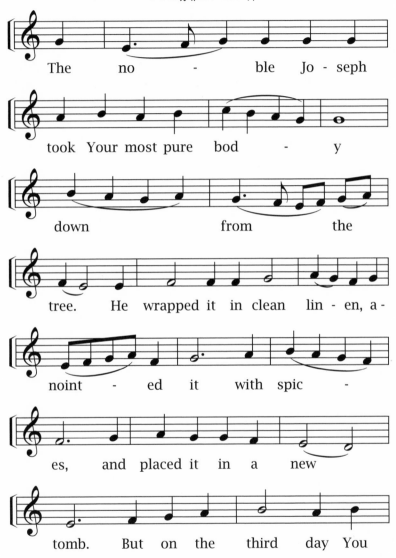

The no - ble Jo - seph took Your most pure bod - y down from the tree. He wrapped it in clean lin - en, a- noint - ed it with spic - es, and placed it in a new tomb. But on the third day You

159

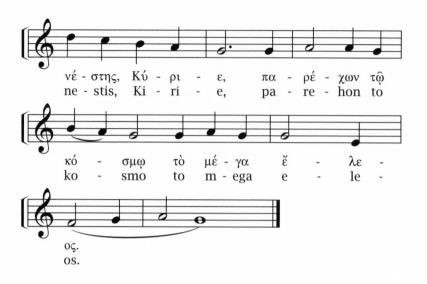

νέ - στης, Κύ - ρι - ε, πα - ρέ - χων τῷ
ne - stis, Ki - ri - e, pa - re - hon to

κό - σμῳ τὸ μέ - γα ἔ - λε -
ko - smo to m-ega e - le -

ος.
os.

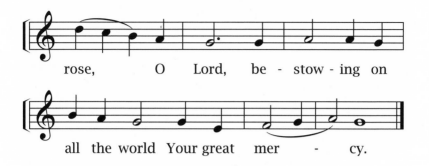

rose, O Lord, be - stow - ing on
all the world Your great mer - cy.

The Sunday of the Myrrh-bearing Women
Another Apolitikion

Ταῖς μυ - ρο - φό - ροις γυ - ναι - ξὶ πα - ρὰ τὸ
Tes mi - ro - fo - ris gi - ne - xi pa - ra to

μνῆ - μα ἐ - πι - στὰς ὁ ἄγ - γε - λος ἐ -
mni - ma e - pi - stas o an - ge - los e -

βό - α· Τὰ
vo - a: Ta

μύ - ρα τοῖς θνη - τοῖς ὑ - πάρ - χει ἀρ -
mi - ra tis thni - tis i - par - hi ar -

μό - δι - α, Χρι - στὸς δὲ δι -
mo - thi - a, Hri - stos the thi -

ἀ φθο - ρᾶς ἐ - δεί - χθη ἀλ - λό - τρι - ος·
a ftho - ras e - thih - thi al - lo - tri - os;

ἀλ - λὰ κραυ - γά - σα - τε· Ἀ -
al - la krav - ga - zon - de: A -

The Sunday of the Myrrh-bearing Women
Another Apolitikion

Ταῖς μυροφόροις γυναιξὶ

The an - gel stood by the

tomb and cried out to the myrrh - bear - ing

wo - men: Myrrh would be fit - ting to a -

noint the dead, but Christ has

shown Him - self to be free from cor -

rup - tion. There-fore, pro - claim that the

Lord is ris - en, be - stow - ing on

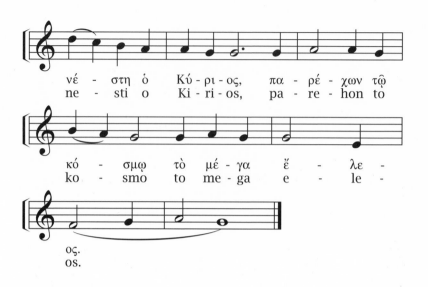

νέ - στη ὁ Κύ - ρι - ος, πα - ρέ - χων τῷ
ne - sti o Ki - ri - os, pa - re - hon to

κό - σμῳ τὸ μέ - γα ἔ - λε -
ko - smo to me - ga e - le -

ος.
os.

all the world His great mer - cy.

Mid-Pentecost/Sunday of the Samaritan Woman
Apolitikion

Με - σού - σης τῆς ἑ - ορ - τῆς, δι -
Me - su - sis tis e - or - tis, thi -

ψώ - σάν μου τὴν ψυ - χήν, εὐ - σε - βεί - ας
pso - san mu tin psi - hin, ef - se - vi - as

πό - τι - σον νά - μα - τα; ὅ - τι
po - ti - son na - ma - ta; o - ti

πᾶ - σι, Σω - τήρ, ἐ - βό - η - σας· Ὁ δι -
pa - si, So - tir, e - vo - i - sas: O thi -

ψῶν ἐρ - χέ - σθω πρός με καὶ πι -
pson er - he - stho pros me ke pi -

νέ - τω. Ἡ πη - γη τῆς ζω - ῆς, Χρι -
ne - to. I pi - gi tis zo - is, Hri -

στὲ ὁ Θε - ός, δό - ξα σοι.
ste o The - os, tho - xa si.

166

Mid-Pentecost/Sunday of the Samaritan Woman
Apolitikion

Μεσούσης τῆς ἑορτῆς

In the midst of this Pas - chal sea - son, Sav - ior, let my thirst - y soul par - take of the wa - ters of true wor - ship; for You call out in - vit - ing all: Let those who thirst come to me and drink. O Foun - tain of Life, Christ our God, glo - ry to You.

The Ascension of the Lord
Apolitikion

'Α - νε - λή - φθης ἐν δό - ξῃ, Χρι - στὲ ὁ Θε -
A - ne - lif - this en tho - xi, Hri - ste o The -

ὸς ἡ - μῶν, χα - ρο - ποι - ή - σας τοὺς μα - θη -
os i - mon, ha - ro - pi - i - sas tus ma - thi -

τὰς τῇ ἐ - παγ - γε - λί - ᾳ τοῦ Ἁ - γί - ου Πνεύ - μα -
tas ti e - pan - ge - li - a tu A - gi - u Pnev - ma -

τος· βε - βαι - ω - θέν των αὐ - τῶν δι - ὰ τῆς εὐ - λο -
tos; ve - ve - o - then ton af - ton thi - s tis ev - li -

γί - ας, ὅ - τι σὺ εἶ ὁ Υἱ - ὸς τοῦ Θε -
gi - as, o - ti si i o I - os tu The -

οῦ, ὁ λυ - τρω - τὴς τοῦ κό - σμου.
u, o li - tro - tis tu ko - smu.

168

The Ascension of the Lord
Apolitikion
᾿Ανελήφθης ἐν δόξῃ

You as - cend-ed in glo - ry, O Christ our

God, hav-ing glad-dened Your dis - ci-ples by Your

prom-ise of the Ho - ly Spir - it. And Your

bless - ing con - firmed their be - lief that

You are in - deed God's Son, the Re -

deem - er of the world.

The Sunday of the Holy Fathers
Apolitikion

Ὑ - περ - δε - δο - ξα - σμέ - νος εἶ Χρι -
I - per - the - tho - xa - sme - nos i Hri -

στὲ ο Θε - ὸς ἡ - μῶν ὁ φω -
ste o The - os i - mon o fo -

στῆ - ρας ἐ - πὶ γῆς τοὺς πα - τέ - ρας ἡ -
sti - ras e - pi gis tus pa - te - ras i -

μῶν θε - με - λι - ώ - σας, καὶ δι᾽ αὐ -
mon the - me - li - o - sas, ke thi' af -

τῶν πρὸς τὴν ἀ - λη - θι - νὴν πί - στιν
ton pros tin a - li - thi - nin pi - stin

πάν - τας ἡ - μᾶς ὁ - δη - γή - σας. Πο - λυ -
pan - das i - mas o - thi - gi - sas. Po - li -

εὐ - σπλαγ - χνε, δό - ξα σοι.
ef - splah - ne, tho - xa si.

170

The Sunday of the Holy Fathers
Apolitikion
Ὑπερδεδοξασμένος εἶ Χριστὲ

Un - end - ing glo - ry be Yours, O Christ our God, for mak - ing our ho - ly fa - thers ra - diant lights to all the world. Through them You led us to the true faith. Com - pas - sion - ate Sav - ior, glo - ry to You.

Pentecost
Apolitikion

Εὐ - λο - γη - τὸς εἶ Χρι - στὲ ὁ Θε -
Ev - lo - yi - tos i Hri - ste o The -

ὸς ἡ - μῶν, ὁ παν - σό - φους
os i - mon, o pan - so - fus

τοὺς ἁ - λι - εῖς ἀ - να - δεί - ξας, κα - τα -
tus a - li - is a - na - thi - xas, ka - ta -

πέμ - ψας αὐ - τοῖς τὸ Πνεῦ - μα τὸ
pem - psas af - tis to Pnev - ma to

Ἅ - γι - ον, καὶ δι' αὐ - τῶν τὴν οἰ - κου -
A - gi - on, ke thi' af - ton tin i - ku -

μέ - νην σα - γη - νεύ - σας. Φι -
me - nin sa - gi - nev - sas. Fi -

λάν - θρω - πε, δό - ξα σοι.
lan - thro - pe, tho - xa si.

Pentecost
Apolitikion

Εὐλογητὸς εἶ Χριστὲ

Bless - ed are You, O Christ our

God. You made wise men of poor

fish - er - men by send - ing down up-

on them Your Ho - ly Spir - it, and through

them You caught the whole world. O

Lov - er of man - kind, glo - ry to You.

The Sunday of All Saints
Apolitikion

Τῶν ἐν ὅ - λῳ τῷ κό - σμῳ μαρ -
Ton en o - lo to ko - smo mar -

τύ - ρων σου, ὡς πορ - φύ - ραν καὶ βύσ - σον τὰ
ti - ron su, os por - fi - ran ke vis - son ta

αἵ - μα - τα ἡ Ἐκ - κλη - σί - α σου στο - λι - σα -
e - ma - ta i Ek - kli - si - a su sto - li - sa -

μέ - νη δι' αὐ - τῶν βο - ᾷ σοι, Χρι -
me - ni thi' af - ton vo - a si, Hri -

στὲ ὁ Θε - ός· Τῷ λα - ῷ σου τους οἰ - κτιρ - μούς
ste o The - os: To la - o su tus i - ktir - mus

σου κα - τά - πεμ - ψον, εἰ - ρή - νην τῇ πο - λι -
su ka - ta - pem - pson, i - ri - nin ti po - li -

τεί - ᾳ σου δώ - ρη - σαι καὶ ταῖς ψυ -
ti - a su tho - ri - se ke tes psi -

χαῖς ἡ - μῶν τὸ μέ - γα ἔ - λε - ος.
hes i - mon to me - ga e - le - os.

174

The Sunday of All Saints
Apolitikion
Τῶν ἐν ὅλῳ τῷ κόσμῳ

Through - out the world Your Church is a -
dorned with the blood of the mar - tyrs
as with roy - al pur - ple and fine
lin - en. Through them she cries out to You,
Christ our God: Grant your last - ing
peace to all the world and be - stow on our
souls Your great mer - cy.

September 8 — The Birth of the Theotokos
Apolitikion

Ἡ γέν-νη - σίς σου, Θε-ο-τό - κε, χα-ρὰν ἐ-
I gen-ni - sis su, The-o - to - ke, ha-ran e-

μύ - νη - σε πᾶ - σι τῇ οἰ - κου -
mi - ni - se pa - si ti i - ku -

μέ-νη· ἐκ σου γὰρ ἀ - νέ-τει-λεν ὁ
me - ni; ek su yar a - ne-ti-len o

Ἥ-λι-ος τῆς δι-και-ο - σύ - νης, Χρι-
I - li-os tis thi-ke-o - si - nis, Hri-

στὸς ὁ Θε - ὸς ἡ-μῶν, καὶ λύ-σας τὴν κα-
stos o The - os i-mon, ke li-sas tin ka-

τά - ραν ἔ - δω-κε τὴν εὐ-λο-
ta - ran e - tho-ke tin ev-lo-

176

September 8 — The Birth of the Theotokos
Apolitikion

Ἡ γέννησίς σου Θεοτόκε

Your birth, O The - o - to - kos, has

filled the world with joy, for there

rose from you the Sun of Jus - tice,

Christ our God. He de - stroyed the

an - cient curse and re - placed it with a

bless - ing, thus con - found-ing death by

giv - ing us e - ter - nal life.

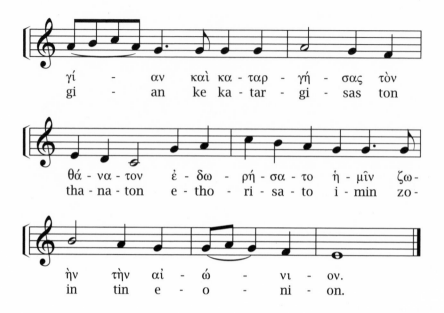

γί - αν καὶ κα - ταρ - γή - σας τὸν
gi - an ke ka - tar - gi - sas ton

θά - να - τον ἐ - δω - ρή - σα - το ἡ - μῖν ζω -
tha - na - ton e - tho - ri - sa - to i - min zo -

ἡν τὴν αἰ - ώ - νι - ον.
in tin e - o - ni - on.

September 14—The Elevation of the Holy Cross
Apolitikion

Σῶ-σον, Κύ - ρι - ε, τὸν λα - όν σου,
So - son, Ki - ri - e, ton la - on su,

καὶ εὐ-λό-γη - σον τὴν κλη - ρο-νο-μί-αν σου,
ke ev - lo - yi - son tin kli - ro-no-mi-an su,

νί - κας τοῖς βα - σι - λεῦ - σι κα-τὰ βαρ-
ni - kas tis va - si - lef - si ka-ta var-
[εὐ - σε - βέ - σι κατ' ἐν - αν-
[ev - se - ve - si kat' en - an-

βά - ρων δω - ροῦ - με - νος,
va - ron tho - ru - me - nos,
τί - ων]
di - on]

καὶ τὸ σὸν φυλ - λάτ - των δι - ὰ τοῦ σταυ-
ke to son fil - lat - ton thi - a tu stav-

ροῦ σου πο - λί - τευ - μα.
ru su po - li - tev - ma.

September 14—The Elevation of the Holy Cross
Apolitikion

Σῶσον Κύριε

Save, O Lord, save Your peo - ple and bless Your in - her - i - tance. Give vic - t'ry to those who bat - tle e - vil and pro - tect us all by Your ho - ly cross.

November 21—The Entry of the Theotokos
Apolitikion

Σή - με - ρον τῆς εὐ - δο - κί - ας Θε -
Si - mer - on tis ev - tho - ki - as The -

οῦ τὸ προ - οί - μι - ον καὶ τῆς τῶν ἀν -
u to pro - i - mi - on ke tis ton an -

θρώ - πων σω - τη - ρί - ας ἡ προ -
thro - pon so - ti - ri - as i pro -

κή - ρυ - ξις; ἐν να - ῷ τοῦ Θε -
ki - ri - xis; en na - o tu The -

οῦ τρα - νῶς ἡ Παρ - θέ - νος
u tra - nos i Par - the - nos

δεί - κνυ - ται καὶ τὸν Χρι-στὸν τοῖς
thi - kni - te ke ton Hri-ston tis

πᾶ - σι προ - κα - ταγ-γέλ - λε - ται. Αὐ -
pa - si pro - ka - tan-gel - le - te. Af -

182

November 21—The Entry of the Theotokos
Apolitikion

Σήμερον τῆς εὐδοκίας Θεοῦ

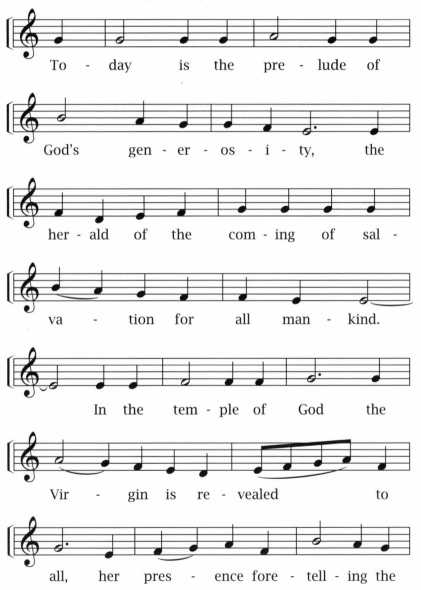

To - day is the pre - lude of

God's gen - er - os - i - ty, the

her - ald of the com - ing of sal -

va - tion for all man - kind.

In the tem - ple of God the

Vir - gin is re - vealed to

all, her pres - ence fore - tell - ing the

τῇ καὶ ἡ - μεῖς με - γα - λο -
ti ke i - mis me - ga - lo -

φώ - νως βο - ή - σω - μεν·
fo - nos vo - i - so - men:

Χαί - ρε, τῆς οἰ - κο - νο - μί - ας τοῦ
He - re, tis i - ko - no - mi - as tu

Κτί - στου ἡ ἐκ - πλή - ρω - σις.
Kti - stu i ek - pli - ro - sis.

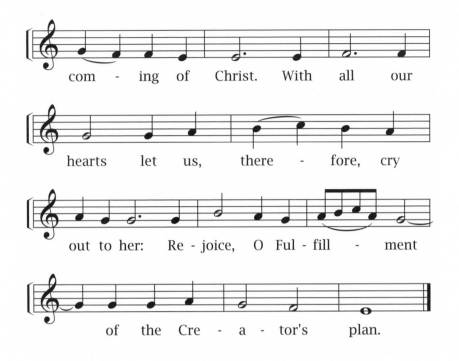

com - ing of Christ. With all our

hearts let us, there - fore, cry

out to her: Re - joice, O Ful - fill - ment

of the Cre - a - tor's plan.

The Sunday of the Ancestors of Christ
Apolitikion

Ἐν πί - στει τοὺς προ - πά - το-ρας ἐ - δι -
En pi - sti tus pro - pa - to-ras e - thi -

καί - ω - σας, τὴν ἐξ' ἐ - θνῶν δι' αὐ -
ke - o - sas, tin ex' e - thnon thi' af -

τῶν προ - μνη - στευ - σά - με - νος Ἐκ - κλη -
ton pro - mni - stev - sa - me - nos Ek - kli -

σί - αν. Καυ - χῶν - ται ἐν
si - an. Kaf - hon - de en

δό - ξῃ οἱ ἅ - γι - οι, ὅ - τι ἐκ
tho - xi i a - gi - i, o - ti ek

σπέρ - μα - τος αὐ - τῶν, υ - πάρ - χει καρ -
sper - ma - tos af - ton, i - par - hi kar -

πός εὐ - κλε - ής, ἡ ἀ -
pos ef - kle - is, i a -

The Sunday of the Ancestors of Christ
Apolitikion
Ἐν πίστει τοὺς προπάτορας

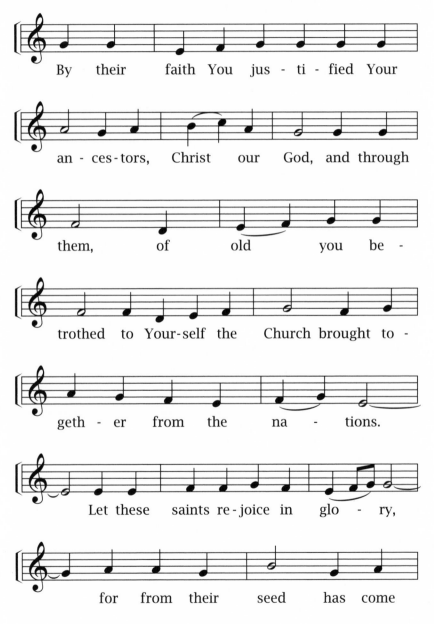

By their faith You jus - ti - fied Your

an - ces - tors, Christ our God, and through

them, of old you be -

trothed to Your-self the Church brought to -

geth - er from the na - tions.

Let these saints re - joice in glo - ry,

for from their seed has come

187

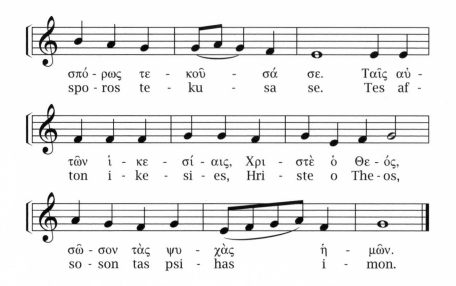

σπό - ρως τε - κοῦ - σά σε. Ταῖς αὐ -
spo - ros te - ku - sa se. Tes af -

τῶν ἱ - κε - σί - αις, Χρι - στὲ ὁ Θε - ός,
ton i - ke - si - es, Hri - ste o The - os,

σῶ - σον τὰς ψυ - χὰς ἡ - μῶν.
so - son tas psi - has i - mon.

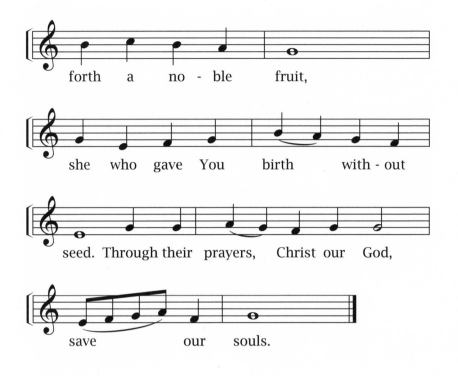

forth a no - ble fruit, she who gave You birth with - out seed. Through their prayers, Christ our God, save our souls.

This commemoration occurs on the Sunday between December 11 and 17, the second Sunday before the Nativity of the Lord.

Preparation of the Nativity (December 20-23)
Apolitikion

Ἑ - τοι - μά - ζου Βη - θλε - έμ, ἤ - νοι - κται
E - ti - ma - zu Vi - thle - em, i - ni - kte

πᾶ - σιν ἡ Ἐ - δέμ· εὐ - τρε - πί - ζου,
pa - sin i E - them; ef - tre - pi - zu,

Ἐ - φρα - θᾶ, ὅ - τι τὸ ξύ - λον τῆς ζω -
E - fra - tha, o - ti to xi - lon tis zo -

ῆς ἐν τῷ σπη - λαί - ῳ ἐ - ξήν - θη - σεν ἐκ τῆς Παρ-
is en to spi - le - o e - xin - thi - sen ek tis Par-

θέ - νου· πα - ρά - δει -
the - nu; pa - ra - thi -

σος καὶ γὰρ ἡ ἐ - κεί - νης γα -
sos ke gar i e - ki - nis ga -

στήρ, ἐ - δεί - χθη νο - η -
stir, e - thih - thi no - i -

190

Preparation of the Nativity (December 20-23)
Apolitikion

Ἐτοιμάζου Βηθλεέμ

Make read - y, Beth - le - hem; O E-den,

o - pen to all. O Eph - ra - tha, pre -

pare, for soon the Tree of

Life will be brought forth from the Vir - gin

in a cave. Like par - a -

dise it - self, she will bear the fruit di -

vine, and if we eat of it,

191

τός, ἐν ᾧ τὸ θεῖ - ον φυ -
tos, en o to thi - on fi -

τόν, ἐξ' οὗ φα - γόν - τες
ton, ex' u fa - gon - des

ζή - σο - μεν, οὐ - χὶ δὲ ὡς ὁ Ἀ -
zi - so - men, u - hi the os o A -

δὰμ τε - θνη - ξό - με - θα.
tham te - thni - xo - me - tha.

Χρι - στὸς γε - νᾶ -
Hri - stos ge - na -

ται, τὴν πρὶν πε - σοῦ - σαν ἀ - να -
te, tin prin pe - su - san a - na -

στή - σων εἰ - κό - να.
sti - son i - ko - na.

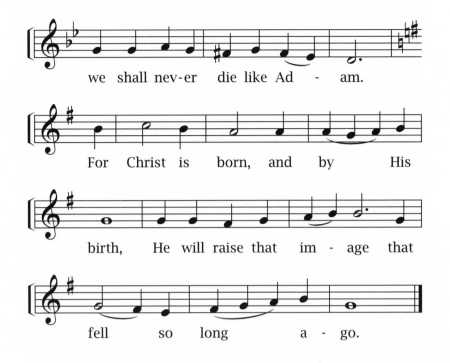

we shall nev-er die like Ad - am.

For Christ is born, and by His

birth, He will raise that im - age that

fell so long a - go.

The Sunday before the Nativity of the Lord
Apolitikion

Με - γά - λα τὰ τῆς πί - στε - ως κα - τορ -
Me - ga - la ta tis pi - ste - os ka - tor -

θώ - μα - τα· ἐν τῇ πη -
tho - ma - ta: en ti pi -

γῇ τῆς φλο - γός, ὡς ἐ - πὶ
gi tis flo - gos, os e - pi

ὕ - δα - τος ἀ - να - παύ - σε - ως, οἱ
i - tha - tos a - na - paf - se - os, i

ἅ - γι - οι τρεῖς παῖ - δες ἠ -
a - gi - i tris pe - thes i -

γάλ - λον - το; καὶ ὁ προ -
gal - lon - do; ke o pro -

φή - της Δα - νι - ήλ, λε - όν - των ποι -
fi - tis Tha - ni - il, le - on - don pi -

The Sunday before the Nativity of the Lord
Apolitikion

Μεγάλα τὰ τῆς πίστεως

How great is the pow'r of faith. By faith three young men re - joice in flames as if in re - fresh - ing wa - ter, and Dan - iel in the li - ons' den is like a shep - herd with his sheep. Through their prayers, Christ our God, save our souls.

μήν, ὡς προ - βά - των ἐ - δεί - κνυ -
min, os pro - va - ton e - thi - kni -

το. Ταῖς αὐ - τῶν ἱ - κε - σί - αις, Χρι -
to. Tes af - ton i - ke - si - as, Hri -

στὲ ὁ Θε - ός, σῶ - σον τὰς ψυ -
ste o The - os, so - son tas psi -

χὰς ἡ - μῶν.
has i - mon.

December 25—The Nativity of the Lord
Apolitikion

Ἡ γέν-νη - σίς σου, Χρι - στὲ ὁ Θε -
I ge - ni - sis su, Hri - ste o The -

ὸς ἡ - μῶν, ἀ - νέ-τει-λε τῷ
os i - mon, a - ne-ti-le to

κό - σμῳ τὸ φῶς τὸ τῆς γνώ - σε -
kos-mo to fos to tis gno - se -

ως, ἐν αὐ - τῇ γὰρ οἱ τοῖς ἄ - στροις λα -
os, en af - ti gar i tis a - stris la -

τρεύ - ον - τες ὑ - πὸ ἀ - στέ - ρος ἐ - δι -
trev - on - des i - po a - ste - ros e - thi -

δά - σκον - το σὲ προσ-κυ - νεῖν τὸν
tha - skon - do se pros-ki - nin ton

Ἥ - λι - ον τῆς δι - και - ο - σύ - νης
i - li - on tis thi - ke - o - si - nis

December 25—The Nativity of the Lord
Apolitikion

Ἡ γέννησίς σου Χριστὲ ὁ Θεὸς ἡμῶν

Your birth, O Christ our

God, shines forth on all the world with the

light of knowl - edge. For

at Your birth, those who had a -

dored the stars were taught by a star to

wor - ship You, to wor - ship

You, the Sun of Jus - tice, and to

199

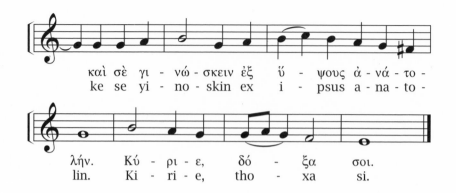

καὶ σὲ γι - νώ - σκειν ἐξ ὕ - ψους ἀ - νά - το -
ke se yi - no - skin ex i - psus a - na - to -

λήν. Κύ - ρι - ε, δό - ξα σοι.
lin. Ki - ri - e, tho - xa si.

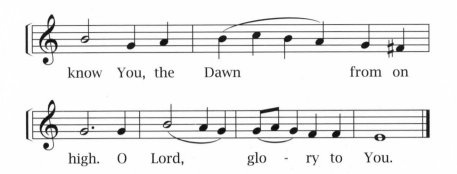

know You, the Dawn from on high. O Lord, glo - ry to You.

The Sunday after the Nativity of the Lord
Apolitikion

Εὐ - αγ - γε - λί - ζου Ἰ - ω - σήφ, τῷ Δαυ - ἰδ τὰ
E - van - ge - li - zu, I - o - sif, to Tha - vid ta

θαύ - μα - τα τῷ Θε - ο - πά - το - ρι· παρ -
thav - ma - ta to the - o - pa - to - ri; par -

θέ - νον εἶ - δες κυ - ο - φο - ρή - σα -
the - non i - thes ki - o - fo - ri - sa -

σαν; με - τὰ ποι - μέ - νων ἐ - δο - ξο - λό - γη - σας·
san; me - ta pi - me - non e - tho - xo - lo - gi - sas;

με - τὰ τῶν μά - γων προ - σε - κύ - νη - σας, δι' ἀγ -
me - ta ton ma - gon pro - se - ki - ni - sas, thi' an -

γέ - λου χρη - μα - τι - σθείς. Ἰ -
ge - lu hri - ma - ti - sthis. I -

κέ - τευ - ε Χρι - στὸν τὸν Θε - ὸν σω -
ke - tev - e Hri - ston ton The - on so -

θῆ - ναι τὰς ψυ - χὰς ἡ - μῶν.
thi - ne tas psi - has i - mon.

202

The Sunday after the Nativity of the Lord
Apolitikion

Εὐαγγελίζου Ἰωσήφ

Go, ho - ly Jo - seph, tell Da - vid what the
an - gel said. With the shep -
herds and the wise men from a -
far, praise the Son of the Vir - gin,
beg - ging Him to save our souls.

Preparation of Theophany (January 2-4)
Apolitikion

Ἑ - τοι - μά - ζου, Ζα - βου - λών, καὶ εὐ-τρε-
E - ti - ma - zu, Za - vu - lon, ke ef-tre-

πί - ζου, Νε - φθα - λήμ, Ἰ - ορ - δά - νη
pi - zu, Ne - ftha - lim, I - or - tha - ni

πο - τα - μέ, στῆ - θι, ὑ - πό-δε-ξαι σκιρ-
po - ta - me, sti - thi, i - po-the-xe skir-

τῶν τοῦ βα - πτι - σθῆ - ναι ἐρ -
ton tu va - pti - sthi - ne er -

χό - με - νον τὸν Δε - σπό - την. Ἀ -
ho - me - non ton The - spo - tin. A -

γάλ - λου ὁ Ἀ - δὰμ σὺν τῇ προ-
gal - lu o A - tham sin ti pro-

μή - το - ρι; μὴ κρύ - πτε - τε ἐ - αυ -
mi - to - ri; mi kri - pte - te e - af-

204

Preparation of Theophany (January 2-4)
Apolitikion

Ἐτοιμάζου Ζαβουλὼν

Make read - y, Zeb - u - lon; pre-pare, O

Neph - tha - li. O Jor - dan, stop your

flow, and with re - joic - ing re-ceive the

Mas - ter as He comes to be bap -

tized. You too, O Ad - am, ex - alt with our

moth - er Eve. Do not hide your -

selves as you did, of old, in par - a -

205

τους ὡς ἐν Πα - ρα - δεί - σῳ τὸ
tus os en Pa - ra - thi - so to

πρίν· καὶ γὰρ γυ - μνοὺς ἰ - δὼν ὑ - μᾶς ἐ -
prin; ke gar gi - mnus i - thon i - mas e -

πέ - φα - νεν, ἵ - να ἐν - δύ - σῃ τὴν
pe - fa - nen, i - na en - thi - si tin

πρώ - την στο - λήν.
pro - tin sto - lin.

Χρι - στὸς ἐ - φά -
Hri - stos e - fa -

νη, τὴν πᾶ - σαν κτί - σιν θέ - λων ἀ -
ni, tin pa - san kti - sin the - lon a -

να - και - νί - σαι.
na - ke - ni - se.

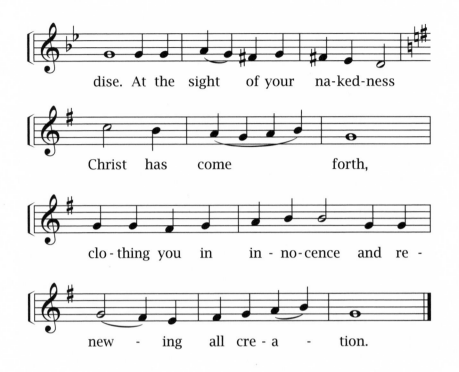

dise. At the sight of your na-ked-ness

Christ has come forth,

clo-thing you in in-no-cence and re-

new - ing all cre-a - tion.

January 6 — Theophany
Apolitikion

Ἐν Ἰ - ορ - δά - νῃ βα-πτι-ζο - μέ - νου σου,
En I - or - tha - ni va-pti-zo - me - nu su,

Κύ-ρι-ε, ἡ τῆς Τρι - ά-δος ἐ-φα-νε - ρώ - θη προ-
Ki-ri-e, i tis Tri - a-thos e-fa-ne - ro - thi pro-

σκύ - νη-σις· τοῦ γὰρ Γεν - νή-το-ρος ἡ φω-
ski - ni-sis; tu gar Yen - ni-to-ros i fo-

νὴ προ-σε-μαρ - τύ - ρει σοι, ἀ - γα-πη -
ni pro-se-mar - ti - ri si, a - ga-pi -

τόν σε Υἱ - ὸν ὀ - νο - μά-ζου-σα καὶ τὸ
ton se I - on o - no - ma-zu-sa ke to

Πνεῦ - μα ἐν εἴ - δει πε - ρι-στε - ρᾶς ἐ - βε -
Pnev - ma en i - thi pe - ri-ste - ras e - ve -

208

January 6—Theophany
Apolitikion
Ἐν Ἰορδάνῃ

At Your bap - ti - sm in the Jor - dan, O Lord, the wor - ship of the Trin - i - ty was made man - i - fest, for the Fa - ther's voice bore You wit - ness by call - ing You his be - lov - ed Son, and the Spir - it in the form of a dove con - firmed the

209

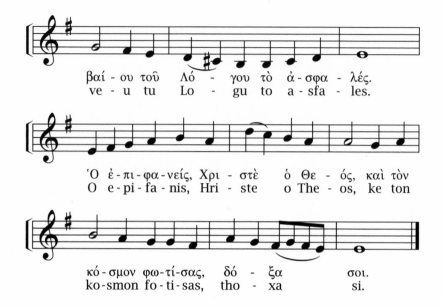

βαί - ου τοῦ Λό - γου τὸ ἀ - σφα - λές.
ve - u tu Lo - gu to a - sfa - les.

Ὁ ἐ - πι - φα - νείς, Χρι - στὲ ὁ Θε - ός, καὶ τὸν
O e - pi - fa - nis, Hri - ste o The - os, ke ton

κό - σμον φω - τί - σας, δό - ξα σοι.
ko - smon fo - ti - sas, tho - xa si.

210

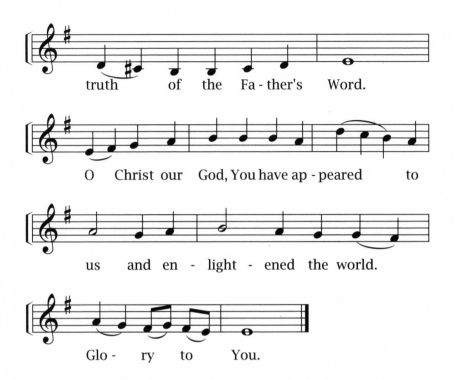

truth of the Fa - ther's Word.

O Christ our God, You have ap - peared to

us and en - light - ened the world.

Glo - ry to You.

February 2 — The Presentation of the Lord
Apolitikion

Χαῖ - ρε κε - χα - ρι - τω - μέ - νη, Θε - ο -
He - re ke - ha - ri - to - me - ni, The - o -

τό - κε Παρ - θέ - νε· ἐκ σοῦ γὰρ ἀ -
to - ke Par - the - ne; ek su gar a -

νέ - τει - λεν ὁ Ἥ - λι - ος τῆς δι - και - ο -
ne - ti - len o I - li - os tis thi - ke - o -

σύ - νης, Χρι - στὸς ὁ Θε - ὸς ἡ - μῶν, φω -
si - nis, Hri - stos o The - os i - mon, fo -

τί - ζων τοὺς ἐν σκό - τει. Εὐ - φραί - νου καὶ
ti - zon tus en sko - ti. Ef - re - nu ke

σὺ πρε - σβύ - τα δί - και - ε, δε -
si pre - svi - ta thi - ke - e, the -

ξά - με - νος ἐν ἀγ - κά - λαις
xa - me - nos en an - ga - les

February 2—The Presentation of the Lord
Apolitikion
Χαῖρε κεχαριτωμένη Θεοτόκε

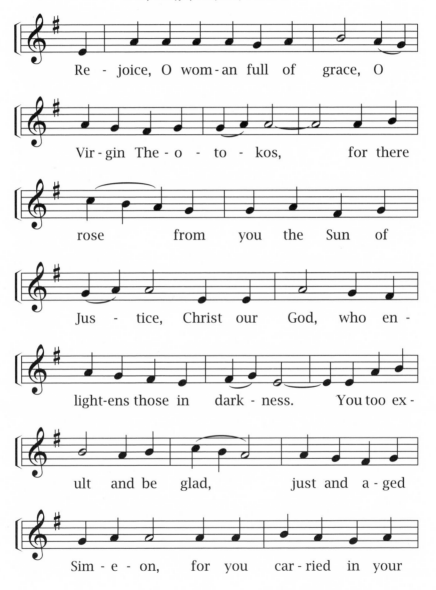

Re - joice, O wom-an full of grace, O Vir-gin The - o - to - kos, for there rose from you the Sun of Jus - tice, Christ our God, who en - light-ens those in dark - ness. You too ex - ult and be glad, just and a - ged Sim - e - on, for you car - ried in your

213

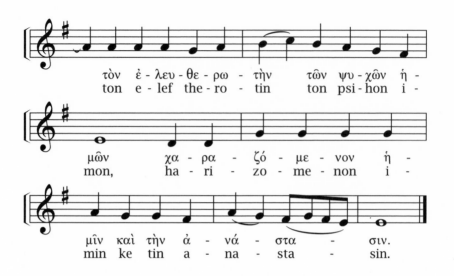

τὸν ἐ - λευ - θε - ρω - τὴν   τῶν ψυ - χῶν ἡ -
ton e - lef the - ro - tin   ton psi - hon i -

μῶν   χα - ρα - ζό - με - νον   ἡ -
mon,   ha - ri - zo - me - non   i -

μῖν καὶ τὴν ἀ - νά - στα - σιν.
min ke tin a - na - sta - sin.

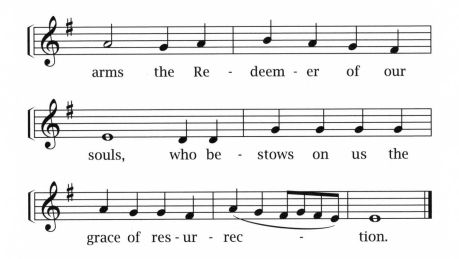

arms the Re - deem - er of our souls, who be - stows on us the grace of res - ur - rec - tion.

March 25—The Annunciation
Apolitikion

Σή - με - ρον τῆς σω - τη - ρί - ας ἡ -
Si - me - ron tis so - te - ri - as i -

μῶν τὸ κε - φά - λαι - ον καὶ τοῦ ἀπ' αἰ -
mon to ke - fa - le - on ke tu ap' e -

ῶ - νος μυ - στη - ρί - ου ἡ φα - νέ - ρω - σις·
o - nos mi - sti - ri - u i fa - ne - ro - sis;

ὁ Υἱ - ὸς τοῦ Θε - οῦ Υἱ -
o I - os tu The - u I -

ὸς τῆς Παρ - θέ - νου γί - νε -
os tis Par - the - nu gi - ne -

ται, καὶ Γα - βρι - ὴλ τὴν χά - ριν εὐ -
te, ke Ga - vri - il tin ha - rin ev -

αγ - γε - λί - ζε - ται. Δι - ὸ καὶ ἡ -
an - ge - li - ze - te. Thi - o ke i -

216

March 25—The Annunciation
Apolitikion
Σήμερον τῆς σωτηρίας ἡμῶν

To - day is the be - gin - ning of

our sal - va - tion and the rev - e -

la - tion of a mys - t'ry which was

hid - den from e - ter - ni - ty. The Son of

God be - comes the Vir - gin's

Son, and Ga - bri - el an - nounc - es the

grace of this Good News. Let us al - so

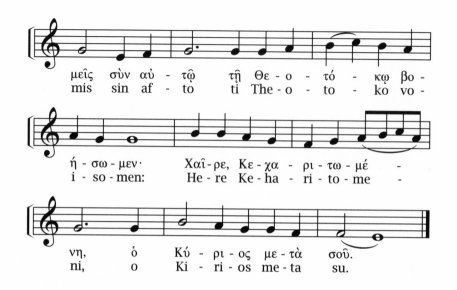

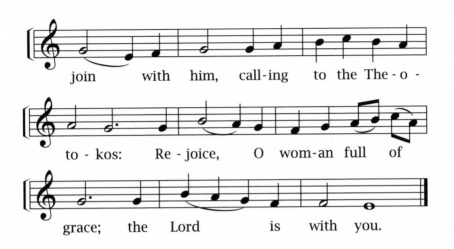

join with him, call-ing to the The-o-to-kos: Re-joice, O wom-an full of grace; the Lord is with you.

August 6—The Transfiguration of the Lord
Apolitikion

Με - τε - μορ - φώ - θης ἐν τῷ ὄ - ρει, Χρι -
Me - te - mor - fo - this en to o - ri, Hri -

στὲ ὁ Θε - ός, δεί - ξας τοῖς
ste o The - os, thi - xas tis

μα - θη - ταῖς σου τὴν δό - ξαν σου κα -
ma - thi - tes su tin tho - xan su, ka -

θὼς ἠ - δύ - ναν - το. Λάμ - ψον καὶ ἡ -
thos i - thi - nan - do. Lam - pson ke i -

μῖν τοῖς ἁ - μαρ - τω - λοῖς τὸ φῶς σου τὸ ἀ -
min tis a - mar - to - lis to fos su to a -

ΐ - δι - ον, πρε - σβεί - αις τῆς Θε - ο - τό - κου·
i - thi - on, pre - svi - es tis The - o - to - ku;

Φω - το - δό - τα, δό - ξα σοι.
Fo - to - tho - ta, do - xa si.

220

August 6—The Transfiguration of the Lord
Apolitikion

Μετεμορφώθης ἐν τῷ ὄρει

When You were trans - fig - ured on the

moun-tain, O Christ our God, You

showed Your dis - ci - ples Your glo - ry as

far as they could bear. So now, for

us sin-ners al - so, let this

same e - ter - nal light shine forth through the

prayers of the The - o - to - kos. O

Giv - er of light, glo - ry to You.

August 15 — The Dormition of the Theotokos
Apolitikion

Ἐν τῇ γεν - νή - σει τὴν παρ - θε -
En ti gen - ni - si tin par - the -

νί - αν ἐ - φύ - λα - ξας, ἐν τῇ κοι -
ni - an e - fi - la - xas, en ti ki -

μή - σει τὸν κό - σμον οὐ κα -
mi - si ton ko - smon u ka -

τέ - λι - πες, Θε - ο - τό - κε. Με -
te - li - pes, The - o - to - ke. Me -

τέ - στης πρὸς τὴν ζω - ήν, μή - τηρ ὑ -
te - stis pros tin zo - in, mi - tir i -

πάρ - χου - σα τῆς ζω - ῆς, καὶ ταῖς πρε -
par - hu - sa tis zo - is, ke tes pre -

σβεί - αις ταῖς σαῖς λυ - τρου - μέ - νη ἐκ θα -
svi - es tes ses li - tru - me - ni ek tha -

νά - του τὰς ψυ - χὰς ἡ - μῶν.
na - tu tas psi - has i - mon.

August 15 — The Dormition of the Theotokos
Apolitikion

Ἐν τῇ γεννήσει

In giv - ing birth you re - mained a

vir - gin, and in your dor - mi - tion

you did not for - sake this world, O The - o -

to - kos. For as the Moth - er of Life,

you have your - self passed in - to life.

And by your prayers you de - liv - er our

souls from death.

KONTAKIA

The Ordinary Kontakion

Προ - στα - σί - α τῶν Χρι - στι - α - νῶν ἀ - κα -
Pro - sta - si - a ton Hri - sti - a - non a - ka -

ταί - σχυν - τε, με - σι - τεί - α πρὸς τὸν ποι - η -
tes - hin - de, me - si - ti - a pros ton pi - i -

τὴν ἀ - με - τά - θε - τε,
tin a - me - ta - the - te,

μὴ πα - ρί - δης ἀ - μαρ - τω -
mi pa - ri - this a - mar - to -

λῶν δε - ή - σε - ων φω - νάς· ἀλ - λὰ
lon the - i - se - on fo - nas; al - la

πρό - φθα - σον, ὡς ἀ - γα - θή, εἰς τὴν βο -
pro - ftha - son, os a - ga - thi, is tin vo -

The Ordinary Kontakion

Προστασία τῶν Χριστιανῶν

O un - fail - ing pro - tec - tion of Chris -

tians, and our faith ful ad - vo - cate be -

fore the Cre - a - tor: though we are

sin - ners, do not ig - nore our en -

treat - y; but in your good - ness, grant your

time-ly help to us who ap - peal to you in

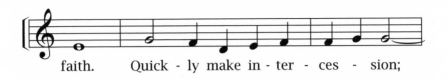

faith.   Quick - ly make in - ter - ces - sion;

on   our   be - half   make   speed-y   sup - pli -

ca - tion,   O   The-o-to - kos,   for   you

al - ways pro - tect those   who   hon-or   you.

September 8—The Birth of the Theotokos
Kontakion

Ἰ - ω - α - κεὶμ καὶ ῎Αν - να ὀ - νει - δι -
I - o - a - kim ke An - na o - ni - thi -

σμοῦ ἀ - τε - κνί - ας καὶ ᾿Α -
smu a - te - kni - as ke A -

δὰμ καὶ Εὔ - α ἐκ τῆς φθο - ρᾶς τοῦ θα -
tham ke Ev - a ek tis ftho - ras tu tha -

νά - του ἠ - λευ - θε - ρώ - θη - σαν,
na - tu i - lef - the - ro - thi - san,

῎Α - χραν - τε, ἐν τῇ ἁ - γί - ᾳ γεν -
A - hran - de, en ti a - gi - a gen -

νή - σει σου. Αὐ - τὴν ἐ - ορ -
ni - si su. Af - tin e - or -

τά - ζει καὶ ὁ λα - ός σου, ἐ - νο -
ta - zi ke o la - os su, e - no -

228

September 8—The Birth of the Theotokos
Kontakion

Ἰωακεὶμ καὶ Ἄννα

Your ho - ly birth de - liv - ered Jo - a - chim and

An - na from the re - proach of

child - less - ness and lib - er - a - ted

Ad - am and Eve from death's cor -

rup - tion, O Pure One. Thus

freed from the stain of sin, we your

peo - ple hon - or your birth, cry - ing

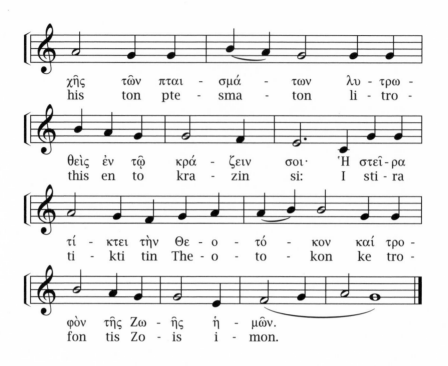

χῆς   τῶν πται - σμά - των   λυ - τρω -
his   ton pte - sma - ton   li - tro -

θεὶς ἐν τῷ   κρά - ζειν   σοι· Ἡ στεῖ - ρα
this en to   kra - zin   si: I sti - ra

τί - κτει τὴν Θε - ο - τό - κον   καί τρο -
ti - kti tin The - o - to - kon ke tro -

φὸν τῆς Ζω - ῆς   ἡ - μῶν.
fon tis Zo - is   i - mon.

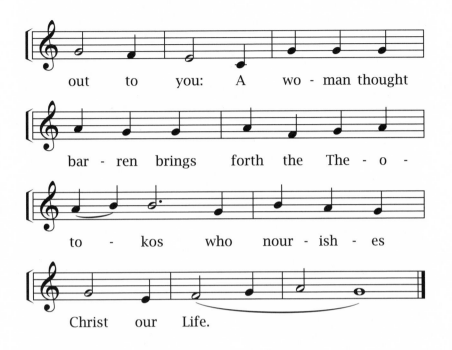

out   to   you: A   wo - man thought

bar - ren   brings   forth   the   The - o -

to - kos   who   nour - ish - es

Christ   our   Life.

September 14—The Elevation of the Holy Cross
Kontakion

Ὁ ὑ - ψω - θεὶς ἐν τῷ σταυ -
O i - pso - this en to stav -

ρῷ ἑ - κου - σί - ως, τῇ ἐ - πω -
ro e - ku - si - os, ti e - po -

νύ - μῳ σου καὶ νῇ πο - λι -
ni - mo su ke ni po - li -

τεί - ᾳ τοὺς οἰ - κτιρ - μούς σου δώ - ρη - σαι, Χρι -
ti - a tus i - ktir - mus su tho - ri - se, Hri -

στὲ ὁ Θε - ός· εὔ - φρα - νον ἐν τῇ δυ -
ste o The - os; ef - ra - non en ti thi -

νά - μει σου τοὺς πι - στοὺς βα - σι -
na - mi su tus pi - stus va - si -

λεῖς ἡ - μῶν, νί - κας χο - ρη - γῶν αὐ -
lis i - mon, ni - kas ho - ri - yon af -

232

September 14—The Elevation of the Holy Cross
Kontakion

Ὁ ὑψωθεὶς

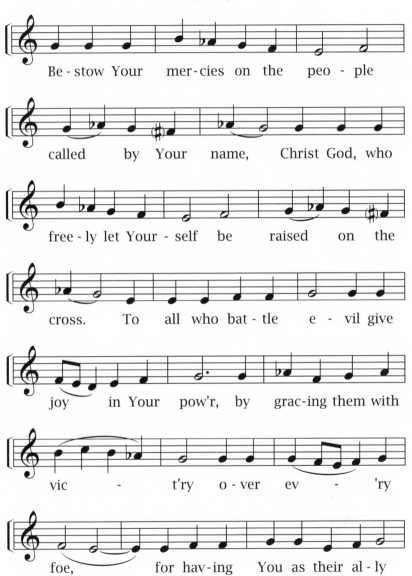

Be - stow Your mer - cies on the peo - ple

called by Your name, Christ God, who

free - ly let Your - self be raised on the

cross. To all who bat - tle e - vil give

joy in Your pow'r, by grac - ing them with

vic - t'ry o - ver ev - 'ry

foe, for hav - ing You as their al - ly

233

τοῖς   κα - τὰ   τῶν   πο - λε - μί -
tis   ka - ta   ton   po - le - mi -

ων.   Τὴν   συμ - μα - χί - αν   ἔ - χοι - εν   τὴν   σὴν
on.   Tin   sim - ma - hi - an   e - hi - en   tin   sin

ὅ - πλον εἰ - ρή - νης,   ἀ - ήτ - τη - τον
o - pon i - ri - nis,   a - it - ti - ton

τρό - παι - ον.
tro - pe - on.

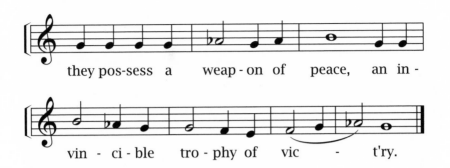

they pos-sess a weap-on of peace, an in-

vin - ci - ble tro - phy of vic - t'ry.

November 21—The Entry of the Theotokos
Kontakion

Ὁ κα - θα - ρώ - τα - τος να -
O ka - tha - ro - ta - tos na -

ὸς τοῦ Σω - τῆ - ρος, ἡ πο - λυ -
os tu So - ti - ros, i po - li -

τί - μη - τος πα - στὰς καὶ παρ -
ti - mi - tos pa - stas ke par -

θέ - νος, τὸ ἱ - ε - ρὸν θη - σαύ - ρι - σμα τῆς
the - nos, to i - e - ron thi - sav - ri - sma tis

δό - ξης τοῦ Θε - οῦ, σή - με - ρον εἰ -
tho - xis tu The - u, si - me - ron i -

σά - γε - ται ἐν τῷ οἴ - κῳ Κυ -
sa - ge - te en to i - ko Ki -

ρί - ου, τὴν χά - ριν συν - ει - σά - γου -
ri - u, tin ha - rin sin - i - sa - gu -

November 21—The Entry of the Theotokos
Kontakion

Ὁ καθαρώτατος ναὸς

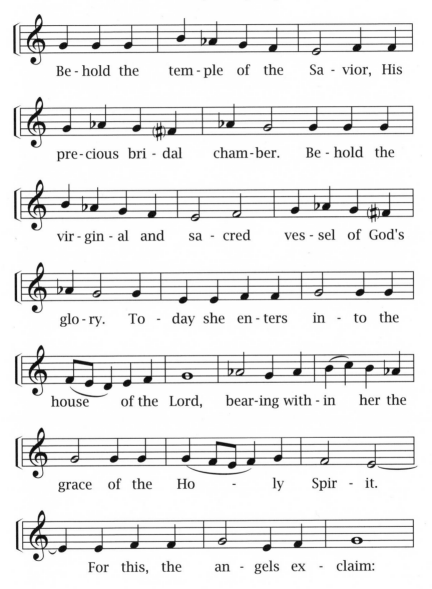

Be - hold the tem - ple of the Sa - vior, His
pre - cious bri - dal cham - ber. Be - hold the
vir - gin - al and sa - cred ves - sel of God's
glo - ry. To - day she en - ters in - to the
house of the Lord, bear-ing with - in her the
grace of the Ho - ly Spir - it.
For this, the an - gels ex - claim:

237

σα   τὴν ἐν   Πνεύ - μα - τι   θεί -
sa   tin en   Pnev - ma - ti   thi -

ῳ·   ἦν   ἀ - νυ - μνοῦ - σιν   ἄγ - γε - λοι Θε - οῦ·
o;   in   a - ni - mnu - sin   an - ge - li The - u:

αὕ - τη ὑ - πάρ - χει   σκη - νὴ   ἐ - που -
af - ti   i - par - hi   ski - ni   e - pu -

ρά   -   νι   -   ος.
ra   -   ni   -   os.

238

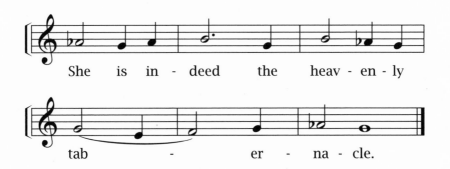

She is in - deed the heav - en - ly

tab - er - na - cle.

Preparation of the Nativity
Kontakion

Ἡ Παρ - θέ - νος σή - με - ρον
I Par - the - nos si - me - ron

τὸν προ - αι - ώ - νι - ον Λό -
ton pro - e - o - ni - on Lo -

γον, ἐν σπη - λαί - ῳ ἔρ - χε - ται
gon, en spi - le - o er - he - te

ἀ - πο - τε - κεῖν ἀ - πορ - ρή - τως.
a - po - te - kin a - po - ri - tos.

Χό - ρευ - ε ἡ οἰ - κου - μέ - νη
Ho - re - ve i i - ku - men - i

ἀ - κου - τι - σθεῖ - σα,
a - ku - ti - sthi - sa,

δό - ξα - σον με - τὰ ἀγ -
tho - xa - zon me - ta an -

Preparation of the Nativity
Kontakion—English

Ἡ Παρθένος σήμερον τὸν προαιώνιον Λόγον

To - day the Vir - gin goes forth,

ma - king her way to a

cave where from her, in - ef - fa - bly,

God the e - ter-nal Word will be born.

Let the world be filled with joy,

hear - ing these ti - dings.

Join - ing the an - gels and

241

γέλ - λων καὶ τῶν ποι - μέ -
ge - lon ke ton pi - me -

νων βου - λη - θέν - τα ἐ - πο -
non vu - li - then - da e - po -

φθῆ - ναι παι - δί - ον νέ -
fthi - ne pe - thi - on ne -

ον τὸν πρὸ αἰ - ώ - νων Θε -
on ton pro e - o - non The -

όν.
on.

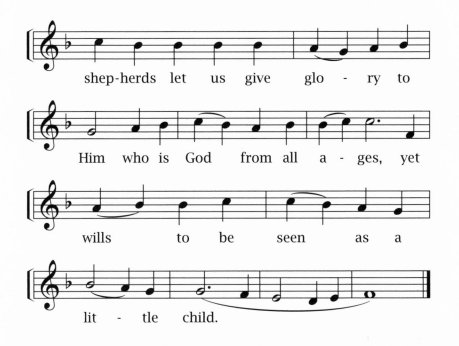

shep-herds let us give glo - ry to

Him who is God from all a - ges, yet

wills to be seen as a

lit - tle child.

December 25—The Nativity of the Lord
Kontakion

Ἡ Παρ - θέ - νος σή - με - ρον
I Par - the - nos si - me - ron

τὸν ὑ - πε - ρού - σι - ον τί -
ton i - pe - ru - si - on ti -

κτει καὶ ἡ γῆ - τὸ σπή - λαι - ον
kti, ke i gi - to spi - le - on

τῷ ἀ - προ - σί - τῳ προ - σά - γει.
to a - pro - si - to pro - sa - gi.

Ἄγ - γε - λοι με - τὰ ποι - μέ - νων
An - ge - li me - ta pi - me - non

δο - ξο - λο - γοῦ - σι,
tho - xo - lo - gu - si,

Μά - γοι δὲ με - τὰ ἀ -
Ma - gi the me - ta a -

244

December 25—The Nativity of the Lord
Kontakion

Ἡ Παρθένος σήμερον τὸν ὑπερούσιον τίκτει

To - day the Vir - gin gives birth

to the Tran - scen - dent

One, and the earth pre - sents a cave

to the Un - ap - proach - a - ble One.

An - gels with shep -

herds give Him glo - ry;

wise men fol - low a

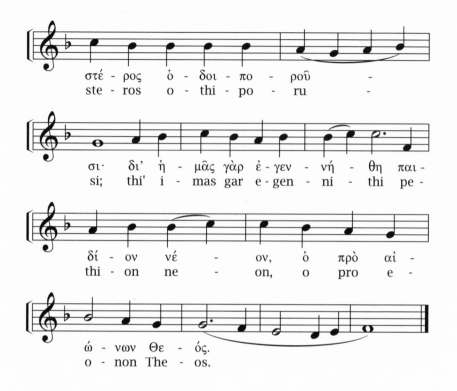

στέ - ρος ὁ - δοι - πο - ροῦ -
ste - ros o - thi - po - ru -

σι· δι᾽ ἡ - μᾶς γὰρ ἐ - γεν - νή - θη παι -
si; thi' i - mas gar e - gen - ni - thi pe -

δί - ον νέ - ον, ὁ πρὸ αἰ -
thi - on ne - on, o pro e -

ώ - νων Θε - ός.
o - non The - os.

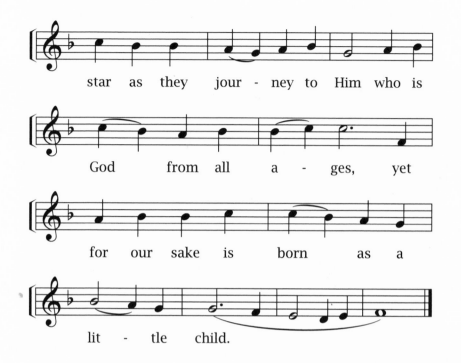

star as they jour - ney to Him who is

God from all a - ges, yet

for our sake is born as a

lit - tle child.

January 6—Theophany
Kontakion

Ἐ - πε - φά - νης σή - με - ρον
E - pe - fa - nis si - me - ron

τῇ οἰ - κου - μέ - νῃ, καὶ τὸ
ti i - ku - me - ni, ke to

φῶς σου, Κύ - ρι - ε,
fos su, Ki - ri - e,

ἐ - ση - μει - ώ - θη ἐφ᾽ ἡ -
e - si - mi - o - thi ef' i -

μᾶς, ἐν ἐ - πι - γνώ - σει ὑ - μνοῦν - τάς σε·
mas, en e - pi - gno - si i - mnun - das se:

Ἦλ - θες ἐ - φά - νης, τὸ
Il - thes, e - fa - nis, to

φῶς τὸ ἀ - πρό - σι - τον.
fos to a - pro - si - ton.

248

January 6—Theophany
Kontakion

Ἐπεφάνης σήμερον

You have re - vealed Your - self to the world to - day, and Your light shines forth on us, who sing Your praise with full knowl - edge: You have come to us, O Lord; You are made man - i - fest, O in - ac - ces - si - ble Light.

February 2 — The Presentation of the Lord

Kontakion

Ὁ μή - τραν παρ - θε - νι - κὴν ἁ - γι -
O mi - tran par - the - ni - kin a - gi -

ἁ - σας τῷ τό - κῳ σου καὶ
a - sas to to - ku su ke

χεῖ - ρας τοῦ Συ - με - ὼν εὐ - λο -
hi - ras tu Si - me - on ev - lo -

γή - σας ὡς ἔ - πρε - πε, προφ -
gi - sas, os e - pre - pe, prof -

θά - σας καὶ νῦν ἔ - σω - σας ἡ - μᾶς, Χρι -
tha - sas ke nin e - so - sas i - mas, Hri -

στὲ ὁ Θε - ός, ἀλλ' εἰ - ρή - νευ - σον
ste o The - os, all' i - ri - nef - son

ἐν πο - λέ - μοις τὸ πο - λί - τευ -
en po - le - mis to pol - li - tev -

250

Ὁ μήτραν παρθενικὴν

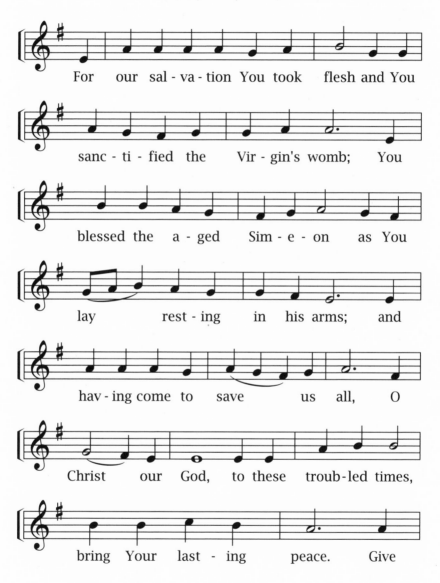

251

APOLITIKIA FROM THE PENTECOSTARION

Pascha
Apolitikion

Χρι - στὸς ἀ - νέ - στη
Hri - stos a - ne - sti

ἐκ νε - κρῶν, θα - νά - τῳ
ek ne - kron, tha - na - to

θά - να - τον πα - τή -
tha - na - ton pa - ti -

σας, καὶ τοῖς ἐν τοῖς
sas, ke tis en tis

μνή - μα - σι ζω - ὴν χα - ρι -
mni - ma - si zo - in ha - ri -

σά - με - νος.
sa - me - nos.

Pascha
Apolitikion
Χριστὸς ἀνέστη

Christ is ri - sen from the

dead, tram - pling down

death by death

and on those in the

grave be - stow - ing

life.

153

Sunday of Thomas — First Sunday after Pascha
Apolitikion

Ἐ - σφρα - γι - σμέ - νου τοῦ
E - sfra - gi - sme - nu tu

μνή - μα - τος, ἡ ζω - ὴ ἐκ τά - φου ἀ -
mni - ma - tos, i zo - i ek ta - fu a -

νέ - τει - λας, Χρι - στὲ ὁ Θε - ός· καὶ τῶν θυ -
ne - ti - las, Hri - ste o The - os; ke ton thi -

ρῶν κε - κλει - σμέ - νων, τοῖς μα - θη - ταῖς ἐ -
ron ke - kli - sme - non, tis ma - thi - tes e -

πέ - στης ἡ πάν - των ἀ - νά - στα - σις,
pe - stis i pan - don a - na - sta - sis,

Πνεῦ - μα εὐ - θὲς δι' αὐ -
Pnev - ma ef - thes thi' af -

154

Sunday of Thomas — First Sunday after Pascha
Apolitikion

Ἐσφραγισμένου τοῦ μνήματος

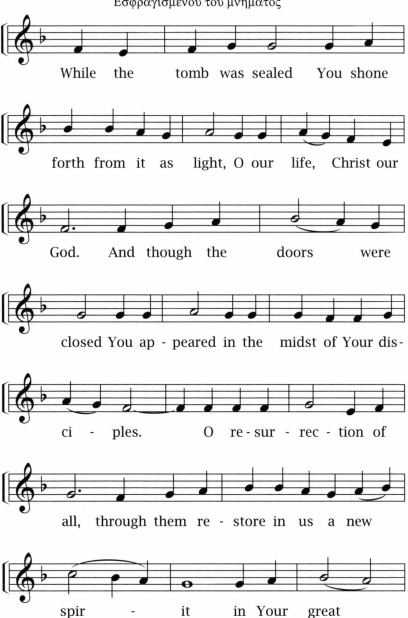

While the tomb was sealed You shone

forth from it as light, O our life, Christ our

God. And though the doors were

closed You ap - peared in the midst of Your dis-

ci - ples. O re - sur - rec - tion of

all, through them re - store in us a new

spir - it in Your great

155

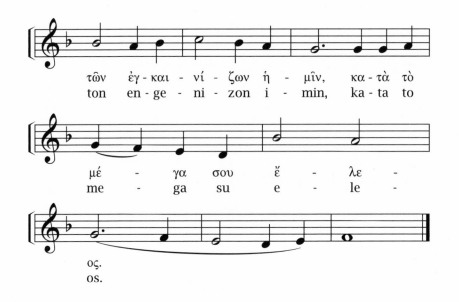

τῶν ἐγ-και - νί - ζων ἡ - μῖν, κα-τὰ τὸ
ton en-ge - ni - zon i - min, ka-ta to

μέ - γα σου ἔ - λε -
me - ga su e - le -

ος.
os.

The Sunday of the Publican and the Pharisee
Kontakion—English

Φαρασαίου φύγωμεν

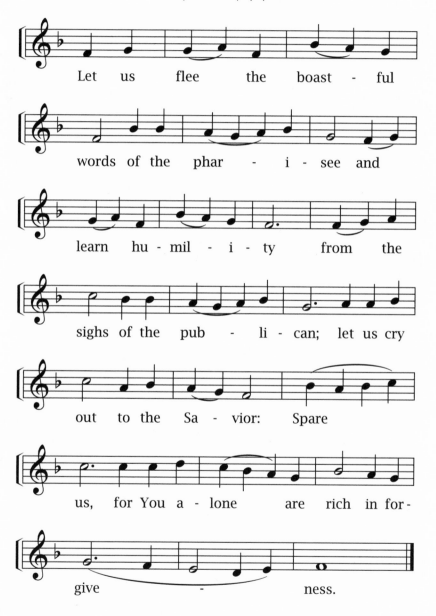

Let us flee the boast - ful

words of the phar - i - see and

learn hu - mil - i - ty from the

sighs of the pub - li - can; let us cry

out to the Sa - vior: Spare

us, for You a - lone are rich in for -

give - ness.

The Sunday of the Prodigal Son
Kontakion

Τῆς πα - τρῴ - ας δό - ξης σου
Tis pa - tro - as tho - xis sou

ἀ - πο - σκιρ - τή - σας ἀ - φρό -
a po - skir - ti - sas a - fro -

νως, ἐν κα - κοῖς ἐ - σκόρ - πι - σα
nos, en ka - kis e - skor - pi - sa

ὅν μοι πα - ρέ - δω - κες πλοῦ - τον·
on mi pa - re - tho - kes plu - ton;

ὅ - θεν σοι τὴν τοῦ ἀ - σώ -
o - then si tin tu a - so -

του φω - νὴν κραυ - γά - ζω·
tu fo - nin krav - ga - zo:

Ἥ - μαρ - τον ἐ - νώ - πι - όν σου,
I - mar - ton e - no - pi - on su,

256

The Sunday of the Prodigal Son
Kontakion—English

Τῆς πατρῴας δόξης

From my Fa - ther's glo - ry

I have fool-ish-ly turned a -

way. By my sins I squan - dered

all the rich-es He gave me.

There - fore like the prod - i - gal I cry

out to Him: I have sinned be-

fore You, com - pas-sion-ate Fa - ther.

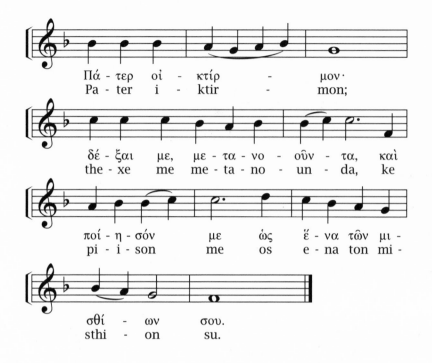

Πά - τερ οἰ - κτίρ - μον·
Pa - ter i - ktir - mon;

δέ - ξαι με, με - τα - νο - οῦν - τα, καὶ
the - xe me me - ta - no - un - da, ke

ποί - η - σόν με ὡς ἕ - να τῶν μι -
pi - i - son me os e - na ton mi -

σθί - ων σου.
sthi - on su.

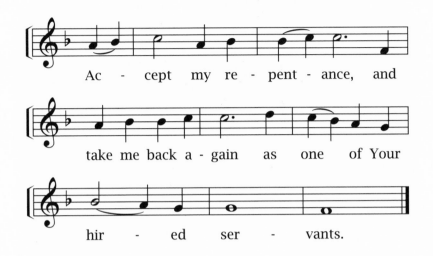

Ac - cept my re - pent - ance, and

take me back a - gain as one of Your

hir - ed ser - vants.

The Sunday of the Last Judgement (Meatfare)
Kontakion

Ὅ - ταν ἔλ - θῃς ὁ Θε -
O - tan el - this o The -

ὸς ἐ - πὶ γῆς με - τὰ δό - ξης, καὶ
os e - pi gis me - ta tho - xis, ke

τρέ - μου - σι τὰ σύμ - παν - τα, πο - τα -
tre - mu - si ta sim - pan - da, po - ta -

μὸς δὲ τοῦ πυ - ρὸς προ τοῦ βή - μα - τος
mos the tu pi - ros pro tu vi - ma - tos

ἔλ - κῃ, καὶ βί - βλοι ἀ - νοί - γων - ται καὶ τὰ κρυ -
el - ki, ke vi - vli a - ni - gon - de ke ta kri -

πτὰ δη - μο - σι - εύ - ων - ται; τό - τε ῥῦ - σαί
pta thi - mo - si - ev - on - de; to - te ri - se

με ἐκ τοῦ πυ - ρὸς τοῦ ἀ - σβέ - στου
me ek tu pi - ros tu a - sve - stu

260

The Sunday of the Last Judgment (Meatfare)
Kontakion
Ὅταν ἔλθῃς

When You come to the earth, O God, in Your glo-ry, all cre - a - tion will trem - ble and a riv - er of fire will flow be - fore Your throne of judg - ment. The books will be o - pened and the se - crets of all will be re - vealed. On that day, O just Judge, de -

261

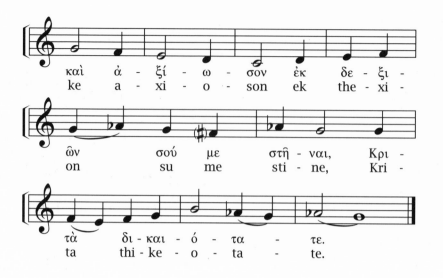

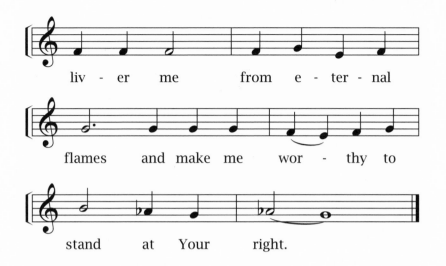

liv - er me from e - ter - nal

flames and make me wor - thy to

stand at Your right.

Forgiveness (Cheesefare) Sunday
Kontakion

Τῆς σο - φί - ας ὁ - δη - γέ, φρο -
Tis so - fi - as o - thi - ge, fro -

νή - σε - ως χο - ρη - γέ, τῶν ἀ -
ni - se - os ho - ri - ge, ton a -

φρό - νων παι - δευ - τά, καὶ τῶν πτω - χῶν ὑ - πε -
fro - non pe - thef - ta, ke ton pto - hon i - pe -

ρα - σπι - στά, στή - ρι - ξον, συν - έ - τι - σον τὴν καρ -
ra - spi - sta, sti - ri - xon, sin - e - ti - son tin kar -

δί - αν μου, Δέ - σπο - τα. Σὺ
thi - an mu, The - spo - ta. Si

δί - δου μοι λό - γον ὁ τοῦ Πα - τρὸς
thi - thu mi lo - gon o tu Pa - tros

Λό - γος· ἰ - δοὺ γὰρ τὰ χεί - λη μου
Lo - gos: i - thu gar ta hi - li mu

264

Forgiveness (Cheesefare) Sunday
Kontakion

Τῆς σοφίας ὁδηγέ

O You who are the source of all wis-dom and dis - cern - ment, in - struc-tor of the ig - no-rant and cham-pion of the poor; strength-en my heart, O Mas - ter, and grant me un - der - stand - ing. O Word of the Fa - ther, bring words to my lips, that noth - ing would

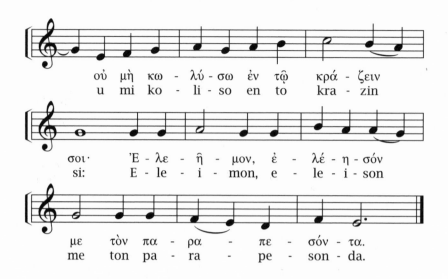

οὐ μὴ κω - λύ-σω ἐν τῷ κρά - ζειν
u mi ko - li - so en to kra - zin

σοι· Ἐ - λε - ῆ - μον, ἐ - λέ - η - σόν
si: E - le - i - mon, e - le - i - son

με τὸν πα - ρα - πε - σόν - τα.
me ton pa - ra - pe - son - da.

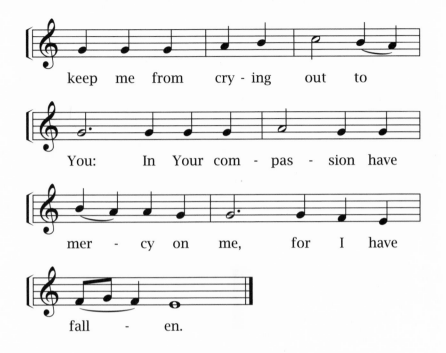

keep me from cry - ing out to You: In Your com - pas - sion have mer - cy on me, for I have fall - en.

March 25—Annunciation
Kontakion

Τῇ ὑ-περ-μά-χῳ στρα-τη-γῷ-τὰ νι-κη-
Ti i-per- ma- ho stra-ti-go-ta ni-ki-

τή-ρι - α. Ὡς λυ-τρω-θεῖ - σα
ti - ri - a. Os li-tro-thi - sa

τῶν δει - νῶν εὐ-χα - ρι - στή - ρι -
ton thi - non ef-ha-ri-sti - ri -

α, ἀ - να-γρά-φω σοι ἡ πό - λις σου,
a, a - na-gra-fo si i po - lis su,

Θε - ο-τό - κε. Ἀλλ' ὡς ἔ - χου-
The - o-to - ke. All' os e - hu -

σα τὸ κρά-τος ἀ-προ-σμά - χη -
sa to kra-tos a-pro-sma - hi -

March 25—Annunciation
Kontakion
Τῇ ὑπερμάχῳ

Vic-tor-ious La - dy, might - y cham-pion, de -

fend - ing us, we your ser - vants

now in - scribe to you this hymn of

thanks, for you res - cued us from

suf-f'ring and trib - u - la - tion. The-o -

to - kos, with your pow - er that can

269

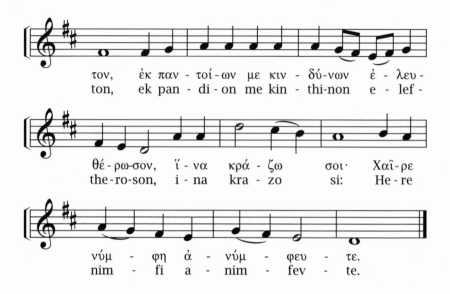

τον, ἐκ παν - τοί - ων με κιν - δύ-νων ἐ - λευ-
ton, ek pan - di - on me kin - thi-non e - lef-

θέ - ρω-σον, ἵ - να κρά - ζω σοι· Χαῖ-ρε
the - ro-son, i - na kra - zo si: He - re

νύμ - φη ἀ - νύμ - φευ - τε.
nim - fi a - nim - fev - te.

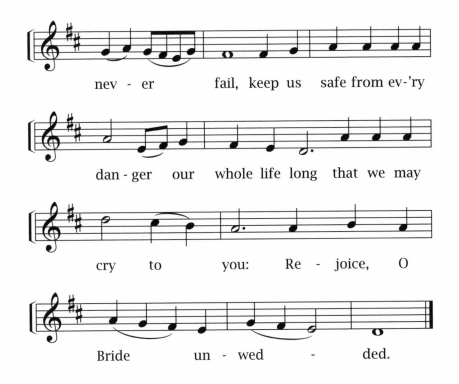

nev - er   fail, keep us   safe from ev-'ry

dan - ger   our   whole life long   that we may

cry   to   you: Re - joice,   O

Bride   un - wed   -   ded.

Palm Sunday
Kontakion

Τῷ θρό - νῳ ἐν οὐ - ρα - νῷ, τῷ
To thro - no en u - ra - no, to

πώ - λῳ ἐ - πὶ τῆς γῆς, ἐ - πο - χού - με - νος, Χρι -
po - lo e - pi tis gis, e - po - hu - me - nos, Hri -

στὲ ὁ Θε - ός, τῶν ἀγ - γέ - λων τὴν
ste o The - os, ton an - ge - lon tin

αἴ - νε - σιν καὶ τῶν παί - δων ἀ - νύ - μνη - σιν προ - σε -
e - ne - sin ke ton pe - thon a - nim - ni - sin pro - se -

δέ - ξω βο - ών - των σοι· Εὐ - λο - γη -
the - xo vo - on - don si: Ev - lo - gi -

μέ - νος ὁ ἐρ - χό - με - νος, τὸν Ἀ -
me - nos o er - ho - me - nos, ton A -

δὰμ ἀ - να - κα - λέ - σα - σθαι.
tham a - na - ka - le - sa - sthe.

272

Palm Sunday
Kontakion—English
Τῷ θρόνῳ ἐν ουρανῷ

In heav - en up - on Your throne, while on

earth rid - ing the colt of a don - key, O

Christ our God, You ac - cept - ed the

an - gels' praise with the songs of the

child - ren who cried out to You: Bless-ed is

He who comes for the res - tor -

a - tion of A - dam.

Pascha
Kontakion

Εἰ καὶ ἐν τά - φῳ κα - τῆλ - θες, ἀ -
I ke en ta - fo ka - til - thes, a -

θά - να - τε, ἀλ - λὰ τοῦ ἅ - δου κα -
tha - na - te, al - la tu a - thu ka -

θεῖ - λες τὴν δύ - να - μιν· καὶ ἀ -
thi - les tin thi - na - min; ke a -

νέ - στης ὡς νι - κη - τής, Χρι - στὲ ὁ Θε -
ne - stis os ni - ki - tis, Hri - ste o The -

ός, γυ - ναι - ξὶ Μυ - ρο - φό - ροις φθεγ -
os, gi - ne - xi Mi - ro - fo - ris ftheng -

ξά - με - νος, χαί - ρε - τε· καὶ τοῖς
xa - me - nos, he - re - te; ke tis

274

Pascha
Kontakion

Εἰ καὶ ἐν τάφῳ

In - to the grave You de - scend - ed, Im -
mor - tal One, yet You de - stroyed the
po - wer of Ha - des, and as
vic - tor You a - rose, O Christ our
God; You pro - claimed to the myrrh - bear - ing
wo - men a greet - ing of joy, You brought
peace to Your ho - ly a - pos -

275

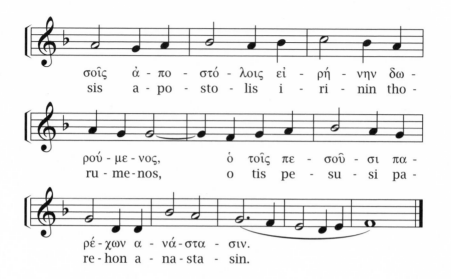

σοῖς ἀ - πο - στό - λοις εἰ - ρή - νην δω -
sis a - po - sto - lis i - ri - nin tho -

ρού - με - νος, ὁ τοῖς πε - σοῦ - σι πα -
ru - me - nos, o tis pe - su - si pa -

ρέ - χων α - νά - στα - σιν.
re - hon a - na - sta - sin.

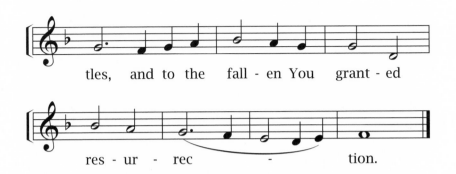

tles,   and to the   fall - en You   grant - ed

res - ur - rec   -   tion.

The Ascension of the Lord
Kontakion

Τὴν ὑ - πὲρ ἡ - μῶν πλη - ρώ - σας οἰ - κο - νο -
Tin i - per i - mon pli - ro - sas i - ko - no -

μί - αν καὶ τὰ ἐ - πὶ γῆς ἐ -
mi - an ke ta e - pi gis e -

νώ - σας τοῖς οὐ - ρα - νί - οις, ἀ - νε -
no - sas tis u - ra - ni - is, a - ne -

λή - φθης ἐν δό - ξῃ, Χρι - στὲ ὁ Θε -
li - fthis en tho - xi, Hri - ste o The -

ὸς ἡ - μῶν, οὐ - δα - μό - θεν χω - ρι -
os i - mon, u - tha - mo - then ho - ri -

ζό - με - νος, ἀλ - λὰ μέ - νων ἀ - δι -
zo - me - nos, al - la me - non a - thi -

ά - στα - τος καὶ βο - ῶν τοῖς ἀ - γα - πῶ-σοί σε· Ἐ -
a - sta - tos ke vo - on tis a - ga - po-si se: E -

γὼ εἰ - μὶ μεθ' ὑ - μῶν, καὶ οὐ - δεὶς καθ' ὑ -
go i - mi meth' i - mon, ke u - this kath' i -

μῶν.
mon.

278

The Ascension of the Lord
Kontakion

Τὴν ὑπὲρ ἡμῶν πληρώσας

When You had joined earth to heav - en and ful - filled Your plan of re - demp - tion, You a - scend - ed in glo - ry, O Christ our God, while re - main - ing in our midst. For You as - sured us who love You that no - one can pre - vail a - gainst us since You Your - self are with us.

Pentecost
Kontakion

Ὅ - τε κα - τα - βὰς τὰς γλώσ - σας συ - νέ - χε -
O - te ka - ta - vas tas glos - sas si - ne - he -

ε, δι - ε - μέ - ρι - ζεν ἔ - θνη ὁ
e, thi - e - me - ri - zen e - thni o

Ὕ - ψι - στος· ὅ - τε τοῦ πυ - ρὸς τὰς
I - psi - stos; o - te tu pi - ros tas

γλώσ - σας δι - έ - νει - μεν, εἰς ἑ -
glos - sas thi - e - ni - men, is e -

νό - τη - τα πάν - τας ἐ - κά - λε -
no - ti - ta pan - das e - ka - le -

σε· καὶ συμ - φώ - νως δο - ξά - ζο -
se; ke sim - fo - nos tho - xa - zo -

μεν τὸ πα - νά - γι - ον
men to pa - na - gi - on

Πνεῦ - μα.
Pnev - ma.

280

Pentecost
Kontakion

Ὅτε καταβὰς τὰς γλώσσας

When He came down and con - fused the

tongues of men, the Most High div -

i - ded the na - tions.

But in send - ing forth part - ed

tongues of flame He called all

man - kind to un - i - ty

that with one ac - cord we might glor - i - fy His

all Ho - ly Spir - it.

The Sunday of All Saints
Kontakion

Ὡς ἀ-παρ-χὰς τῆς φύ-σε-ως τῷ φυ-τουρ-
Os a-par-has tis fi-se-os to fi-tur-

γῷ τῆς κτί-σε-ως ἡ οἰ-κου-
go tis kti-se-os i i-ku-

μέ-νη προ-σφέ-ρει σοι, Κύ-ρι-ε,
me-ni pro-sfe-ri si, Ki-ri-e,

τοὺς θε-ο-φό-ρους μάρ-τυ-
tus the-o-fo-rus mar-ti-

ρας. Ταῖς αὐ-τῶν ἱ-κε-σί-αις ἐν εἰ-
ras. Tes af-ton i-ke-si-es en i-

ρή-νη βα-θεί-ᾳ τὴν Ἐκ-κλη-σί-αν
ri-ni va-thi-a tin Ek-kli-si-an

σου, δι-ὰ τῆς Θε-ο-τό-κου συν-
su, thi-a tis The-o-to-ku sin-

τή-ρη-σον πο-λυ-έ-λε-ε.
di-ri-son po-li-e-le-e.

282

The Sunday of All Saints
Kontakion—English
Ὡς ἀπαρχὰς τῆς φύσεως

To You, O Lord, Cre - a - tor of the u - ni - verse, the world of - fers the God - bear - ing mar - tyrs as the first fruits of cre - a - tion. Through their prayers, and through those of the The - o - to - kos, keep Your Church in per - fect peace, O Sa - vior rich in mer - cy.

August 6—The Transfiguration of the Lord
Kontakion

Ἐ - πὶ τοῦ ὄ - ρους με - τε - μορ -
E - pi tu o - rus me - te - mor -

φώ - θης, καὶ ὡς ἐ -
fo - this, ke os e -

χώ - ρουν οἱ μα - θη - ταί σου τὴν
ho - run i ma - thi - te su tin

δό - ξαν σου, Χρι - στὲ ὁ Θε -
tho - xan su, Hri - ste o The -

ός, ἐ - θε - ά - σαν - το, ἵ - να
os, e - the - a - san - do, i - na

ὅ - ταν σὲ ἴ - δω - σι σταυ -
o - tan se i - tho - si stav -

ρού - με - νον, τὸ μὲν πά - θος νο -
ru - me - non, to men pa - thos no -

August 6—The Transfiguration of the Lord
Kontakion

Ἐπὶ τοῦ ὄρους μετεμορφώθης

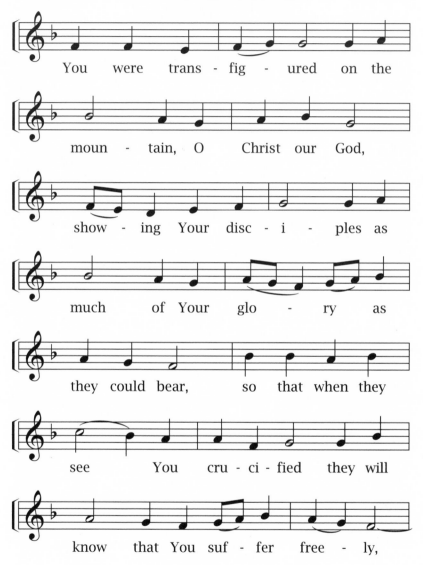

You were trans - fig - ured on the

moun - tain, O Christ our God,

show - ing Your disc - i - ples as

much of Your glo - ry as

they could bear, so that when they

see You cru - ci - fied they will

know that You suf - fer free - ly,

ἡ - σω - σιν ἐ - κού - σι - ον, τῷ δὲ
i - so - sin e - ku - si - on, to the

κό - σμῳ κη - ρύ - ξω -
ko - smo ki - ri - xo -

σιν ὅ - τι σὺ ὑ - πάρ - χεις ἀ - λη -
sin o - ti si i - par - his a - li -

θῶς τοῦ Πα - τρὸς τὸ ἀ -
thos tu Pa - tros to a -

παύ - γα - σμα.
pav - ga - sma.

and they will tell all the

world that You are tru - ly the

ra - diance of the Fa - ther.

August 15 — The Dormition of the Theotokos
Kontakion

Τὴν ἐν πρε - σβεί - αις α - κοί - μη - τον
Tin en pre - svi - es a - ki - mi - ton

Θε - ο - τό - κον καὶ προ - στα -
The - o - to - kon ke pro - sta -

σί - αις ἀ - με - τά - θε - τον ἐλ -
si - es a - me - ta - the - ton el -

πί - δα, τά - φος καὶ νέ - κρω - σις
pi - tha, ta - fos ke ne - kro - sis

οὐκ ἐ - κρά - τη - σεν; ὡς γὰρ Ζω -
uk e - kra - ti - sen; os gar Zo -

ῆς Μη - τέ - ρα πρὸς τὴν ζω - ὴν με -
is Mi - te - ra pros tin zo - in me -

τέ - στη - σεν, ὁ μή - τραν οἰ -
te - sti - sen, o mi - tran i -

κή - σας ἀ - ει - πάρ - θε - νον.
ki - sas a - i - par - the - non.

August 15 — The Dormition of the Theotokos
Kontakion

Τὴν ἐν πρεσβείαις

She is our vig - i - lant in - ter - ces - sor, the The - o - to - kos, our sure hope and pro - tec - tion. Neith - er death nor tomb held an - y pow - er o - ver her, for as the Moth - er of Life, she was ta - ken in - to life by that ver - y one who deigned to dwell in her ev - er vir - gin womb.

INSTEAD OF THE TRISAGION HYMN

On September 14 and the Third Sunday of Great Lent

Τὸν σταυ - ρόν σου προ-σκυ-νοῦ - μεν,
Ton stav - ron su pros-ki - nu - men,

Δέ - σπο - τα, καὶ τὴν ἁ - γί - αν σου ἀ -
The - spo - ta, ke tin a - gi - an su a -

νά - στα-σιν δο - ξά - ζο - μεν.(3)
na - sta-sin tho - xa - zo - men.(3)

Δό - ξα Πα-τρὶ καὶ Υἱ - ῷ καὶ Ἁ-γί-ῳ Πνεύ-μα-τι· καὶ
Tho - xa Pa - tri ke I - o ke A-yi-o Pnev-ma-ti; ke

νῦν καὶ ἀ-εὶ καὶ εἰς τοὺς αἰ-ῶ-νας τῶν αἰ - ώ-νων. Ἀ - μήν.
nin ke a-i ke is tus e-o-nas ton e - o-non. A - min.

Καὶ τὴν ἁ - γί - αν σου ἀ - νά - στα-
Ke tin a - gi - an su a - na - sta-

σιν δο - ξά - ζο - μεν.
sin tho - xa - zo - men.

Priest: Δύναμις.
We repeat: Τὸν σταυρόν σου...

290

INSTEAD OF THE TRISAGION HYMN

On September 14 and the Third Sunday of Great Lent

Be - fore Your cross we bow down, O

Mas - ter, and we glo - ri - fy Your

ho - ly res - ur - rec - tion.(3)

Glo-ry to the Fa-ther and the Son and the Ho-ly Spir-it, now and

ev - er and to the a - ges of a - ges. A - men.

And we glo - ri - fy Your

ho - ly res - ur - rec - tion.

Priest: Again, fervently.
We repeat: Before Your cross...

291

INSTEAD OF THE TRISAGION HYMN

Lazarus Saturday, Pascha and New Week
Pentecost and the day following
The Nativity and the day following (12/25; 12/26)
Epiphany and the day following (1/6; 1/7)

῞Ο - σοι εἰς Χρι - στὸν ἐ - βα - πτί - σθη - τε Χρι -
O - si is Hri - son e - va - pti - sthi - te Hri -

στὸν ἐ - νε - δύ - σα - σθε. ᾿Αλ - λη - λού - ϊ - α.(3)
ston e - ne - thi - sa - sthe. Al - li - lu - i - a.(3)

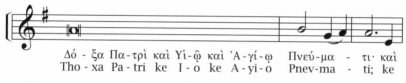

Δό - ξα Πα - τρὶ καὶ Υἱ - ῷ καὶ ᾿Α - γί - ῳ Πνεύ - μα - τι καὶ
Tho - xa Pa - tri ke I - ó ke A - yi - o Pnev - ma - ti; ke

νῦν καὶ ἀ - εὶ καὶ εἰς τοὺς αἰ - ῶ - νας τῶν αἰ - ώ - νων. ᾿Α - μήν.
nin ke a - i ke is tus e - o - nas ton e - o - non. A - min.

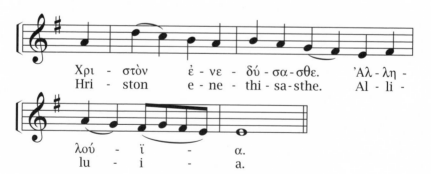

Χρι - στὸν ἐ - νε - δύ - σα - σθε. ᾿Αλ - λη -
Hri - ston e - ne - thi - sa - sthe. Al - li -

λού - ϊ - α.
lu - i - a.

Priest: Δύναμις.
We repeat: ῞Οσοι εἰς Χριστόν...

292

INSTEAD OF THE TRISAGION HYMN

Lazarus Saturday, Pascha and the New Week
Pentecost and the day following
Christmas and the day following (12/25, 12/26)
Epiphany and the day following (1/6, 1/7)

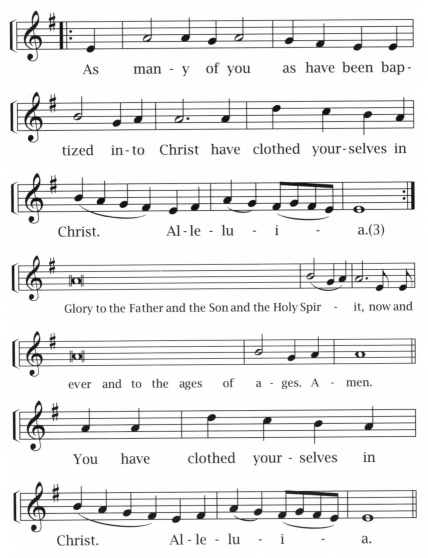

As man-y of you as have been bap-tized in-to Christ have clothed your-selves in Christ. Al-le-lu-i-a.(3)

Glory to the Father and the Son and the Holy Spir - it, now and ever and to the ages of a - ges. A - men.

You have clothed your - selves in Christ. Al-le-lu - i - a.

Priest: Again, fervently.
We repeat: As many of you...

293

ALTERNATE CHERUBIC HYMN

'Α - μήν. Οἱ τὰ χε - ρου - βεὶμ
A - min. I ta he - ru - vim

μυ - στι - κῶς εἰ - κο - νί - ζον -
mi - sti - kos i - ko - ni - zon -

τες καὶ
des ke

τῇ ζω - ο - ποι - ῷ
ti zo - o - pi - o

Τρι - ά - δι,
Tri - a - thi,

Τρι - ά - δι τὸν τρι-
Tri - a - thi ton tri-

σά - γι - ον ὕ - μνον προ - σά - δον - τες,
sa - gi - on i - mnon pro - sa - thon - des,

294

ALTERNATE CHERUBIC HYMN

A - men. Let   us who mys-tic'-lly re-pre-sent the

cher-u - bim,   re-pre-sent   the cher-u-

bim,   and sing   the thrice   ho - ly

hymn, sing the thrice   ho - ly   hymn

to   the life giv-ing Trin   -   i - ty,

sing   the thrice   ho - ly hymn to   the life giv-ing

Trin - i - ty,   to   the life giv-ing Trin - i- ty,

πᾶ - σαν τὴν βι - ο - τι - κὴν ἀ - πο-
pa - san tin vi - o - ti - kin a - po-

θώ - με - θα, πᾶ - σαν μέ - ρι - μναν
tho - me - tha, pa - san me - ri - mnan

ὡς τὸν βα - σι - λέ - α τῶν
os ton va - si - le - a ton

ὅ - λων ὑ - πο - δε - ξό - με - νοι... Ἀ - μήν.
o - lon i - po - the - xo - me - ni... A - min.

ταῖς ἀγ - γε - λι - καῖς ἀ - ο - ρά -
tes an - ge - li - kes a - o - ra -

τως δο - ρυ - φο - ρού - με - νον τά - ξε -
tos tho - ri - fo - ru - me - non ta - xe -

σιν. Ἀλ - λη - λού - ϊ - α.(3)
sin. Al - li - lu - i - a.(3)

296

set a - side all cares of life, all

cares of life, all cares of life

that we may re - ceive the King of

all, re-ceive the King of all... A - men.

in - vis - i - bly es - cort - ed, es - cort -

ed by the an - gel - ic hosts, by the an-

gel - ic hosts. Al-le - lu - i - a.(3)

MEGALYNARIA

At the Liturgy of St. Basil

Megalynarion

Ἐ-πὶ σοὶ χαί-ρει κε-χα - ρι-τω-μέ-νη πᾶ - σα ἡ
E - pi si he - ri ke-ha - ri-to-me-ni pa - sa i

κτί - σις, ἀγ - γέ - λων τὸ σύ-στη-μα καὶ ἀν-
kti - sis, an - ge - lon to si - sti-ma ke an-

θρώ - πων τὸ γέ - νος. Ἡ-γι - α - σμέ-νε να-
thro - pon to ge - nos. I - gi - a - sme-ne na-

ἐ καὶ πα - ρά - δει-σε λο-γι-κέ, παρ-θε-νι-
e ke pa - ra - thi-se lo-gi-ke, par-the-ni-

κὸν καύ-χη - μα, ἐξ ἧς Θε - ὸς ἐ-σαρ-
kon kaf-hi - ma, ex is The - os e - sar-

κώ - θη καὶ παι - δί - ον γέ - γο - νεν ὁ πρὸ αἰ-
ko - thi ke pe - thi-on ge-go - nen o pro e-

ώ - νων ὑ - πάρ - χων Θε - ὸς ἡ - μῶν.
o - non i - par - hon The - os i - mon.

298

At the Liturgy of St. Basil
Megalynarion

Ἐπὶ σοὶ χαίρει

In you, O wo-man full of grace, all cre-a-tion re-joic-es, the or-ders of an-gels and the race of man-kind. O hal-low'd tem - ple and spir-it-u-al par-a-dise, glo-ry of vir-gin-al souls, from you our God was in-car-nate and be-came a child, He who is God from all a - ges.

Τὴν γὰρ σὴν μή - τραν θρό -
Tin gar sin mi - tran thro -

νον ἐ ποί - η - σε καὶ τὴν σὴν γα-στέ -
non e pi - i - se ke tin sin ga-ste -

ρα πλα-τυ - τέ - ραν
ra pla-ti - te - ran

οὐ - ρα - νῶν ἀ -πειρ-γά - σα - το.
u - ra - non a -pir-ga - sa - to.

Ἐ - πὶ σοὶ χαί - ρει κε-χα-
E - pi si he - ri ke-ha-

ρι - τω - μέ - νη
ri - to - me - ni

πᾶ - σα ἡ κτί -
pa - sa i kti -

σις, δό - ξα σοι.
sis, tho - xa si.

By mak - ing your womb His

throne He made

you more spa -

cious, more spa - cious than

all the heav - ens.

In you, O

wo - man full of grace all cre -

a - tion, all cre - a - tion re -

joic - es. Glo - ry to you.

Palm Sunday
Megalynarion

Θε - ὸς Κύ - ρι - ος καὶ ἐ - πέ - φα - νεν ἡ -
The - os Ki - ri - os ke e - pe - fa - nen i -

μῖν. Συ - στή - σα - σθε ἐ - ορ - τὴν καὶ ἀ - γαλ -
min. Si - sti - sa - sthe e - or - tin ke a - gal -

λό - με - νοι δεῦ - τε με - γα - λύ - νω - μεν Χρι -
lo - me - ni thef - te me - ga - li - no - men Hri -

στόν, με - τὰ βα - ΐ - ων καὶ κλά - δων
ston, me - ta va - i - on ke kla - thon

ὕ - μνοις κραυ - γά - ζον - τες· Εὐ - λο - γη -
im - nis krav - ga - zon - des: Ev - lo - gi -

μέ - νος ὁ ἐρ - χό - με - νος ἐν ὀ - νό - μα - τι Κυ -
me - nos o er - ho - me - nos en o - no - ma - ti Ki -

ρί - ου, Σω - τῆ - ρος ἡ - μῶν.
ri - u, So - ti - ros i - mon.

302

Palm Sunday
Megalynarion

Θεὸς Κύριος

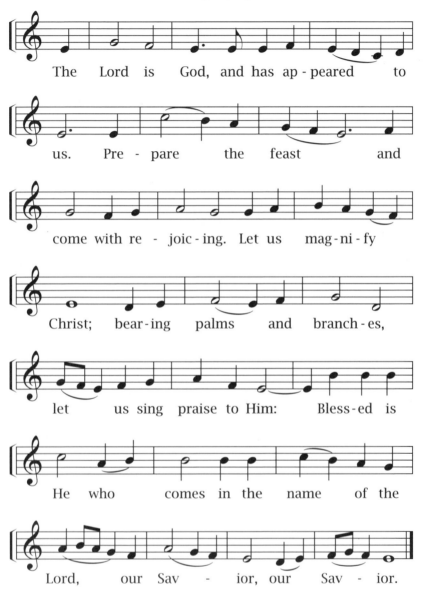

The Lord is God, and has ap - peared to us. Pre - pare the feast and come with re - joic - ing. Let us mag - ni - fy Christ; bear - ing palms and branch - es, let us sing praise to Him: Bless - ed is He who comes in the name of the Lord, our Sav - ior, our Sav - ior.

Pascha

Megalynarion

Ὁ ἄγ - γε - λος ἐ - βό - α τῇ
O an - ge - los e - vo - a ti

κε - χα - ρι - τω - μέ - νῃ· ἁ - γνὴ Παρ - θέ - νε,
ke - ha - ri - to - me - ni: a - gni Par - the - ne,

χαῖ - ρε, καὶ πά - λιν ἐ - ρῶ χαῖ - ρε, ὁ
he - re, ke pa - lin e - ro he - re, o

σὸς Υἱ - ὸς ἀ - νέ - στη τρι -
sos I - os a - ne - sti tri -

ἡ - με - ρος ἐκ τά - φου. Φω -
i - me - ros ek ta - fu. Fo -

τί - ζου, φω - τί - ζου, ἡ
ti - zu, fo - ti - zu, i

νέ - α Ἱ - ε - ρου - σα - λήμ, ἡ γὰρ
ne - a I - e - ru - sa - lim, i gar

304

Pascha
Megalynarion
Ὁ ἄγγελος ἐβόα

The an-gel cried out to the wom - an

full of grace: Re - joice, O pure Vir - gin; a -

gain I say, re - joice, for your Son is

ris - en from the tomb on the

third day. Shine, shine, O

new Je - ru - sa - lem, for the

glo - ry of the Lord has

δό - ξα Κυ - ρί - ου ἐ - πὶ
tho - xa Ki - ri - u e - pi

σὲ ἀ - νέ - τει - λε. Χό - ρευ - ε
se a - ne - ti - le. Ho - rev - e

νῦν καὶ ἀ - γάλ - λου Σι - ών.
nin ke a - gal - lou Si - on.

Σὺ - δὲ ἀ - γνή, τέρ - που, Θε - ο -
Si - the, a - gni ter - pou, The - o -

τό - κε, ἐν τῇ ἐ - γέρ - σει τοῦ
to - ke, en ti e - ger - si tu

τό - κου σου.
to - ku su.

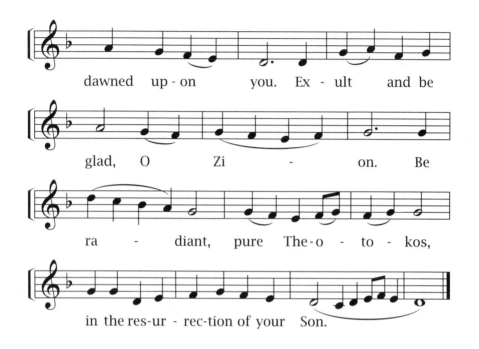

dawned up-on you. Ex - ult and be

glad, O Zi - on. Be

ra - diant, pure The-o - to - kos,

in the res-ur - rec-tion of your Son.

The Sunday of St. Thomas
Megalynarion

Σὲ τὴν φα - ει - νὴν λαμ - πά - δα καὶ μη -
Se tin fa - i - nin lam - ba - tha ke mi -

τέ - ρα τοῦ Θε - οῦ, τὴν ἀ -
te - ra tu The - u, tin a -

ρί - ζη - λον δό - ξαν καὶ ἀ - νω -
ri - zi - lon tho - xan ke a - no -

τέ - ραν πάν - των τῶν ποι - η -
te - ran pan - don ton pi - i -

μά - των, ἐν ὕ -
ma - ton, en i -

μνοις με - γα - λύ - νο - μεν.
mnis me - ga - li - no - men.

The Sunday of St. Thomas
Megalynarion

Σὲ τὴν φαεινύν λαμπάδα

You are the shin-ing light and the Moth - er of God, of in - com - p'ra - ble glo - ry and high - er in dig-ni - ty than all crea - tures; with songs of praise we mag - ni-fy you.

Pentecost
Megalynarion

Μὴ τῆς φθο - ρᾶς δι - α - πεί - ρα κυ - ο - φο-
Mi tis ftho - ras thi - a - pi - ra ki - o - fo-

ρή - σα - σα καὶ παν - τε - χνή - μο - νι
ri - sa - sa ke pan - de - hni - mo - ni

Λό - γῳ σάρ - κα δα - νεί - σα - σα,
Lo - go sar - ka tha - ni - sa - sa,

μῆ - τερ ἀ - πεί - ραν - δρε, Παρ - θέ - νε Θε - ο-
mi - ter a - pi - ran - thre, Par - the - ne The - o-

τό - κε, δο - χεῖ - ον τοῦ ἀ - στέ - κτου, χω-
to - ke, tho - hi - on tu a - ste - ktu, ho-

ρί - ον τοῦ ἀ - πεί - ρου πλα - στουρ - γοῦ σου,
ri - on tu a - pi - ru pla - stur - gu su,

σὲ με - γα - λύ - νο - μεν.
se me - ga - li - no - men.

310

Pentecost
Megalynarion
Μὴ τῆς φθορᾶς

You con - ceived and gave birth in vir-

gin - i - ty; the Word who cre - a - ted all, through

you be-came in - car - nate. O Moth - er who

knew not man, Vir-gin The-o - to - kos, the

bound - less One was held by you, the

dwell - ing of your in - fin - ite Cre -

a - tor; we mag-ni - fy you.

December 25—The Nativity of the Lord
Megalynarion

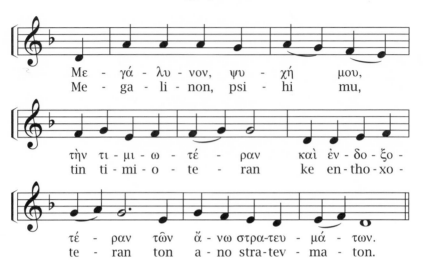

Με - γά - λυ - νον, ψυ - χή μου,
Me - ga - li - non, psi - hi mu,

τὴν τι - μι - ω - τέ - ραν καὶ ἐν - δο - ξο -
tin ti - mi - o - te - ran ke en - tho - xo -

τέ - ραν τῶν ἄ - νω στρα-τευ - μά - των.
te - ran ton a - no stra-tev - ma - ton.

Μυ - στή - ρι - ον
Mi - sti - ri - on

ξέ - νον ὁ - ρῶ καὶ πα - ρά - δο -
xe - non o - ro ke pa - ra - tho -

ξον· οὐ - ρα - νὸν τὸ σπή-λαι-ον· θρό - νον χε -
xon: u - ra - non to spi - le - on; thro-non he -

ρου - βι - κὸν τὴν Παρ - θέ - νον· τὴν
ru - vi-kon tin Par - the - non; tin

December 25—The Nativity of the Lord
Megalynarion

Μεγάλυνον ψυχή μου τὴν τιμιωτέραν

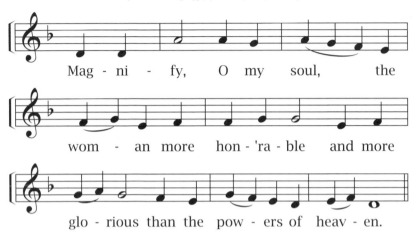

Mag - ni - fy, O my soul, the

wom - an more hon - 'ra - ble and more

glo - rious than the pow - ers of heav - en.

I see a

mys - t'ry, strange

and most won - drous: The

cave has be - come heav - en, the

φάτ - νην χω - ρί - ον· ἐν ᾧ ἀ - νε -
fat - nin ho - ri - on; en o a - ne -

κλή - θη ὁ ἀ - χώ - ρη - τος, Χρι - στὸς ὁ Θε -
kli - thi o a - ho - ri - tos, Hri - stos o The -

ός, ὃν ἀ - νυ - μνοῦν - τες με - γα -
os, on a - ni - mnun - des me - ga -

λύ - νο - μεν.
li - no - men.

Vir - gin, the throne of the cher - u - bim. The man - ger holds Him who can - not be held or con - tained, Christ our God, whom we praise and mag - ni - fy.

COMMUNION HYMNS

Saturday of Lazarus
Communion Hymn: Psalm 8

in Greek

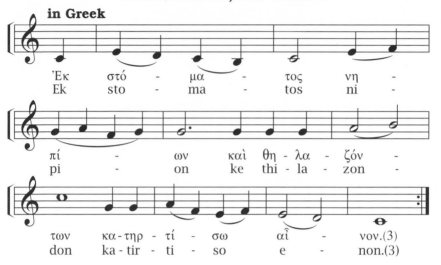

Ἐκ στό - μα - τος νη -
Ek sto - ma - tos ni -

πί - ων καὶ θη - λα - ζόν -
pi - on ke thi - la - zon -

των κα - τηρ - τί - σω αἶ - νον.(3)
don ka - tir - ti - so e - non.(3)

or, in English

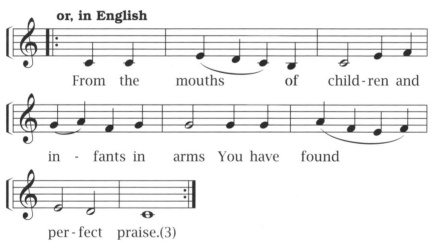

From the mouths of child-ren and

in - fants in arms You have found

per - fect praise.(3)

Conclusion

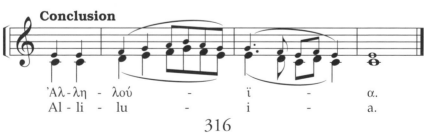

Ἀλ - λη - λού - ϊ - α.
Al - li - lu - i - a.

316

Palm Sunday
Communion Hymn: Psalm 117 [118]

in Greek

Εὐ-λο-γη-μέ - νος ὁ ἐρ-χό-με - νος ἐν ὀ-νό-μα-τι Κυ-ρί - ου, βα-σι-λεὺς τοῦ Ἰ-σρα-ήλ.(3)

Ev-lo-gi-me - nos o er-ho-me - nos en o-no-ma-ti Ki-ri - u, va-si-lefs tu I-sra-il.(3)

or, in English

Bless-ed is He who comes in the name of the Lord, bless-ed is He who comes in the name of the Lord, the King of Is-ra - el.(3)

Conclusion

Ἀλ-λη-λού - ï - α.

Al-li-lu - i - a.

317

Pascha
Communion Hymn

in Greek

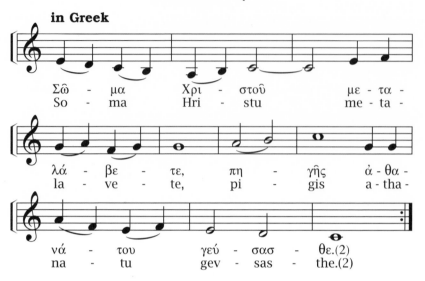

Σῶ - μα   Χρι - στοῦ   με - τα -
So - ma   Hri - stu   me - ta -

λά - βε - τε,   πη - γῆς   ἀ - θα -
la - ve - te,   pi - gis   a - tha -

νά - του   γεύ - σασ - θε.(2)
na - tu   gev - sas - the.(2)

or, in English

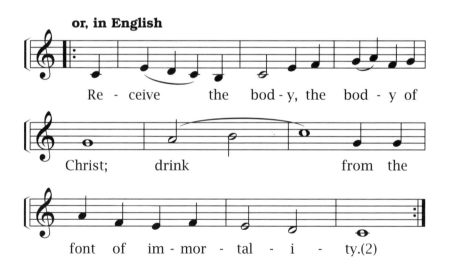

Re - ceive   the   bod - y, the   bod - y of

Christ;   drink   from   the

font   of   im - mor - tal - i - ty.(2)

Concluding repetition

Σῶ - μα   Χρι - στοῦ   με - τα -
So - ma   Hri - stu   me - ta -

λά - βε - τε,   πη - γῆς
la - ve - te,   pi - gis

πη - γῆς   πη -
pi - gis   pi -

γῆς   ἀ - θα -
gis   a - tha -

νά - του   γεύ - σασ - θε.   Ἀλ - λη -
na - tu   gev - sas - the.   Al - li -

λού - ϊ - α.
lu - i - a.

319

Sunday of Thomas—First Sunday after Pascha
Communion Hymn: Psalm 147 [147B]

in Greek

Ἐ - παί - νει Ἰ - ε - ρου - σα - λὴμ τὸν
E - pe - ni I - e - ru - sa - lim ton

Κύ - ρι - ον· αἴ - νει
Ki - ri - on; e - ni

αἴ - νει τὸν Θε - όν σου, Σι - ών.(3)
e - ni ton The - on su, Si - on.(3)

or, in English

Ex - alt in the Lord, O Je -

ru - sa - lem; praise your God, praise your

God, O Zi - on.(3)

Conclusion

Ἀλ - λη - λού - ϊ - α.
Al - li - lu - i - a.

320

The Ascension of the Lord
Communion Hymn: Psalm 46 [47]

in Greek

Ἀ - νέ - βη ὁ Θε - ὸς ἐν ἀ-
A - ne - vi o The - os en a-

λα - λαγ - μῷ, Κύ - ρι - ος, ἐν φω - νῇ, ἐν φω-
la - lag - mo, Ki - ri - os, en fo - ni, en fo-

νῇ σάλ - πιγ - γος.(3)
ni sal - pin - gos.(3)

or, in English

God a - scends a - mid shouts of

joy; the Lord goes up, the Lord goes

up to the sound of the trum - pet.(3)

Conclusion

Ἀλ - λη - λού - ï - α.
Al - li - lu - i - a.

321

Pentecost
Communion Hymn: Psalm 142 [143]

in Greek

Tò πνεῦ - μά σου τò ἀ - γα -
To pnev - ma su to a - ga -

θòν ὁ - δη - γή - σει με ἐν γῇ, ἐν
thon o - thi - gi - si me en gi, en

γῇ εὐ - θεί - ᾳ.(3)
gi ev - thi - a.(3)

or, in English

Let Your good Spi - rit lead

me a - long a path that is sure, a

path that is sure and straight.(3)

Conclusion

'Αλ - λη - λού - ï - α.
Al - li - lu - i - a.

322

The Sunday of All Saints
Communion Hymn: Psalm 32 [33]

in Greek

Ἀ - γαλ - λι - ᾶ - σθε   δί - και - οι
A - gal - li - a - sthe   thi - ke - i

ἐν Κυ - ρί - ῳ·   τοῖς εὐ - θέ -
en Ki - ri - ò;   tis ev - the -

σι   πρέ - πει   αἴ - νε - σις.(3)
si   pre - pi   e - ne - sis.(3)

or, in English

Ex - alt, you   just,   in the   Lord.   Ex -

alt, you   just, in the   Lord; from the   up -

right   praise   is   fit - ting.(3)

Conclusion

Ἀλ - λη - λού - ϊ - α.
Al - li - lu - i - a.

323

September 8—The Birth of the Theotokos
Communion Hymn: Psalm 115 [116]

in Greek

Πο - τή - ρι - ον σω - τη - ρί - ου
Po - ti - ri - on so - ti - ri - u

λή - ψο - μαι καὶ τὸ ὄ - νο - μα Κυ -
li - pso - me ke to o - no - ma Ki -

ρί - ου ἐ-πι-κα - λέ - σο - μαι.(3)
ri - u e-pi-ka - le - so - me.(3)

or, in English

I will lift the cup, lift the cup of sal-

va - tion, I will lift the cup of sal-

va - tion and call on the name of the Lord.(3)

Conclusion

'Αλ - λη - λού - ϊ - α.
Al - li - lu - i - a.

324

September 14—The Exaltation of the Holy Cross
Communion Hymn: Psalm 4

in Greek

Ἐ - ση - μει - ώ - θη ἐφ' ἡ - μᾶς τὸ
E - si - mi - o - thi ef' i - mas to

φῶς τοῦ προ - σώ - που σου,
fos tu pro - so - pu su,

Κύ - ρι - ε, Κύ - ρι - ε.(3)
Ki - ri - e, Ki - ri - e.(3)

or, in English

Let the light of Your face

shine on us, let the light of Your face

shine on us, O Lord.(3)

Conclusion

Ἀλ - λη - λού - ϊ - α.
Al - li - lu - i - a.

325

December 25—The Nativity of the Lord
Communion Hymn: Psalm 110 [111]

in Greek

Λύ - τρω - σιν ἀ - πέ - στει - λε
Li - tro - sin a - pe - sti - le

Κύ - ρι - ος τῷ λα - ῷ,
Ki - ri - os to la - o

τῷ λα - ῷ αὐ - τοῦ.(3)
to la - o af - tu.(3)

or, in English

The Lord has sent re - demp -

tion, the Lord has sent re - demp -

tion to His peo - ple.(3)

Conclusion

'Αλ-λη - λού - ϊ - α.
Al - li - lu - i - a.

January 6—Theophany
Communion Hymn

in Greek

Ἐ - πε - φά - νη ἡ χά - ρις
E - pe - fa - ni i ha - ris

τοῦ Θε - οῦ, ἡ σω - τή - ρι - ος
tu The - u, i so - ti - ri - os

πᾶ - σιν ἀν - θρώ - ποις.(3)
pa - sin an - thro - pis.(3)

or, in English

The grace of God, the grace of

God has ap - peared, for the sal - va -

tion of all peo - ple.(3)

Conclusion

Ἀλ - λη - λού - ϊ - α.
Al - li - lu - i - a.

327

January 7—St. John the Forerunner and Baptist
Communion Hymn: Psalm 111 [112]

in Greek

Εἰς μνη - μό - συ - νον αἰ -
Is mni - mo - si - non e -

ὥ - νι - ον ἔ - σται,
o - ni - on e - ste,

ἔ - σται δί - και - ος.(3)
e - ste thi - ke - os.(3)

or, in English

The mem - 'ry of the right -

eous will en - dure, en -

dure for - ev - er.(3)

Conclusion

Ἀλ - λη - λού - ϊ - α.
Al - li - lu - i - a.

328

March 25—The Annunciation
Communion Hymn: Psalm 131 [132]

in Greek

Ἐ - ξε - λέ - ξα - το Κύ - ρι - ος τὴν Σι -
E - xe - le - xa - to Ki - ri - os tin Si -

ών, ἠ - ρε - τί - σα το αὐ - τὴν
on, i - re - ti - sa to af - tin

εἰς κα - τοι - κί - αν ἐ - αυ - τῷ.(3)
is ka - ti - ki - an e - af - to.(3)

or, in English

The Lord has cho - sen, has cho - sen

Zi - on; He has de - sired

it for His hab - i - ta - tion.(3)

Conclusion

Ἀλ - λη - λού - ϊ - α.
Al - li - lu - i - a.

329

August 6—The Transfiguration of the Lord
Communion Hymn: Psalm 88 [89]

in Greek

Ἐν τῷ φω - τὶ τῆς δό - ξης τοῦ προ -
En to fo - ti tis tho - xis tu pro -

σώ - που σου, Κύ - ρι - ε, πο - ρευ -
so - pu su, Ki - ri - e, po - rev -

σό - με - θα εἰς τὸν αἰ - ῶ - να.(3)
so - me - tha is ton e - o - na.(3)

or, in English

We will walk in the light, we will walk in the

light of the glo - ry of Your

face, O Lord, for - ev - er.(3)

Conclusion

Ἀλ - λη - λού - ϊ - α.
Al - li - lu - i - a.

HYMNS FOR OTHER DIVINE SERVICES

Vespers 332
Hierarchical Services 343
Salutations/Akathist Hymn . . 344
Pascha: Before the Service at Midnight 348
Wedding Service 350
Services For the Departed . . . 354

VESPERS
At the Offering of Incense

ʾΗχος Α'

'Α - μήν. Κύ - ρι - ε ἐ - κέ - κρα -
A - min. Ki - ri - e e - ke - kra -

ξα πρὸς σέ, εἰ - σά - κου -
xa pros se, i - sa - ku -

σόν μου· εἰ - σά - κου -
son mu; i - sa - ku -

σόν μου, Κύ - ρι - ε.
son mu, Ki - ri - e.

Κύ - ρι - ε ἐ - κέ - κρα - ξα πρὸς
Ki - ri - e e - ke - kra - xa pros

σέ, εἰ - σά - κου - σόν μου
se, i - sa - ku - son mu

πρό - σχες τῇ φω - νῇ τῆς δε -
pros - hes ti fo - ni tis the-

ή - σε - ώς μου
i - se - os mu

332

VESPERS
At the Offering of Incense

Κύριε ἐκέκραξα

Tone 1

A - men.   O   Lord, I call up - on You,

hear   me;   hear   me, O

Lord.   O   Lord, I call up - on   You,

hear   me;   hear my voice when I

cry   out   to   You.

Hear   me,   hear

me,   O   Lord. Let my   prayer

ἐν τῷ κε-κρα-γέ-ναι με πρὸς σέ· εἰ-
en to ke-kra-ge-ne me pros se; i-

σά - κου-σόν μου, Κύ - ρι -
sa - ku-son mu, Ki - ri -

ε. Κα-τευ-θυν-θή - τω ἡ προ - σευ-
e. Ka-tev-thin-thi - to i pro - sef-

χή μου ὡς θυ-μί-α-μα ἐ-
hi mu os thi-mi-a-ma e-

νώ-πι-όν σου ἔ-παρ-σις
no-pi-on su e-par-sis

τῶν χει-ρῶν μου θυ-σί-α ἐ-
ton hi-ron mu thi-si-a e-

σπε-ρι-νή· εἰ-σά-κου-σόν μου,
spe-ri-ni; i-sa-ku-son mu,

Κύ - ρι - ε.
Ki - ri - e

rise like in - cense be - fore

You, the lift - ing up of my

hands like the eve - ning sac - ri -

fice. Hear me,

hear me, O Lord.

VESPERS
Daily Hymn

Φῶς ἱ-λα-ρὸν ἁ-γί-ας δό - ξης, ἀ-θα-
Fos i-la-ron a-gi-as tho - xis, a-tha-

νά - του Πα-τρός, οὐ-ρα-νί - ου, ἁ-
na - tu Pa-tros, u-ra-ni - u, a-

γί-ου μά-κα - ρος, Ἰ-η-σοῦ Χρι -
gi-u, ma-ka - ros, I-i-su Hri -

στέ, ἐλ - θόν - τες ἐ-πὶ
ste, el - thon - des e-pi

τὴν ἡ-λί-ου δύ - σιν, ἰ-δόν-τες
tin i-li-u thi - sin, i-thon-des

φῶς ἑ-σπε-ρι - νόν, ὑ - μνοῦ-μεν Πα-
fos e-spe-ri - non, i - mnu-men Pa-

336

VESPERS
Daily Hymn
Φῶς ἱλαρὸν

Ra - diant Light of the ho - ly glo -

ry of the im - mor - tal ho - ly,

heav - en - ly and bless - ed Fa - ther, O

Christ Je - sus. Now as we

come to the sun - set, as we

see the eve - ning light, we sing to

τέ - ρα, Υἱ - όν, καὶ Ἅ - γι - ον
te - ra, I - on, ke A - gi - on

Πνεῦ - μα, Θε - όν. Ἄ - ξι - όν σε ἐν
Pnev - ma, The - on. A - xi - on se en

πᾶ - σι και - ροῖς, ὑ - μνεῖ - σθαι φω -
pa - si ke - ris, i - mni - sthe fo -

ναῖς αἰ - σί - αις, Υἱ - ὲ Θε -
nes e - si - es, I - e The -

οῦ, ζω - ὴν ὁ δι -
u, zo - in o thi -

δούς· Δι - ὸ ὁ κόσ - μος
thus. Thi - o o kos - mos

σὲ δο - ξά - ζει.
se tho - xa - zi.

338

God   the   Fa - ther,   Son,   and

Ho - ly Spi - rit.   At   all   times are You

wor - thy   to   be   praised   by

un - de - filed   tongue,   O   Son   of

God,   who give   life   to   the

world.   For   this   the   whole world

glo - ri - fies   You.

VESPERS

Prokimenon for Saturday evening: Psalm 92[93]

in Greek

'Ο Κύ - ρι - ος ἐ - βα - σί - λευ - σεν, εὐ -
O Ki - ri - os e - va - si - lef - sen, ef -

πρέ - πει - αν ἐ - νε - δύ - σα - το.
pre - pi - an e - ne - thi - sa - to.

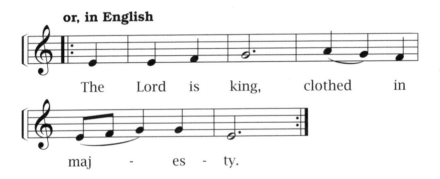

or, in English

The Lord is king, clothed in

maj - es - ty.

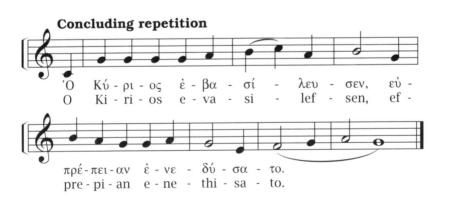

Concluding repetition

'Ο Κύ - ρι - ος ἐ - βα - σί - λευ - σεν, εὐ -
O Ki - ri - os e - va - si - lef - sen, ef -

πρέ - πει - αν ἐ - νε - δύ - σα - το.
pre - pi - an e - ne - thi - sa - to.

VESPERS

On the evening of Pascha, Sunday of Orthodoxy and Pentecost

Great Prokimenon: Psalm 76[77]

in Greek

Τίς Θε - ὸς μέ - γας ὡς
Tis The - os me - gas os

ὁ Θε ὸς ἡ - μῶν· σὺ εἶ ὁ Θε-
o The os i - mon; si i o The -

ὸς ὁ ποι ῶν θαυ - μά - σι - α μό νος.
os o pi - on thav - ma - si - a mo nos.

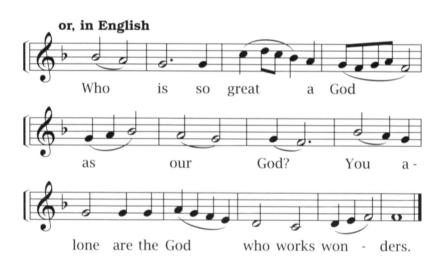

or, in English

Who is so great a God

as our God? You a -

lone are the God who works won - ders.

VESPERS
At the Blessing of Bread

in Greek

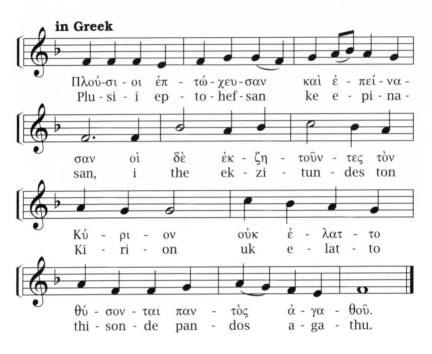

Πλού-σι - οι ἐπ - τώ-χευ-σαν καὶ ἐ - πεί - να -
Plu - si - i ep - to-hef-san ke e - pi - na -

σαν οἱ δὲ ἐκ - ζη - τοῦν - τες τὸν
san, i the ek - zi - tun - des ton

Κύ - ρι - ον οὐκ ἐ - λατ - το
Ki - ri - on uk e - lat - to

θύ - σον - ται παν - τὸς ἀ - γα - θοῦ.
thi - son - de pan - dos a - ga - thu.

or, in English

Man - y who are wealth-y suf - fer

hun - ger and need, but those who

seek the Lord nev - er stand in

want of a - ny bless - ing.

342

Τὸν δεσ - πό - την καὶ ἀρ - χι - ε -
Ton thes - po - tin ke ar - hi - e -

ρέ - α ἡ - μῶν, Κύ - ρι - ε,
re - a i - mon, Ki - ri - e,

φύ-λατ-τε. Εἰς πολ - λά ἔ - τη, δέσ - πο - τα. Εἰς πολ-
fi - lat - te. Is pol - la e - ti, thes-po - ta. Is pol -

λά ἔ - τη, δέσ-πο-τα. Εἰς πολ - λά ἔ - τη,
la e - ti, thes-po - ta. Is pol - la e - ti,

δέσ - πο - τα.
thes - po - ta.

Grant long life, Lord, to our master and hierarch.

ΧΑΙΡΕΤΙΣΜΟΙ / SALUTATIONS SERVICE

(Τῇ ὑπερμάχῳ / Victorious Lady: *see pages 268/269)*

344

ΧΑΙΡΕΤΙΣΜΟΙ / SALUTATIONS SERVICE

(Τῇ ὑπερμάχῳ / Victorious Lady: *see pages 268/269*)

First Response

Re - joice, O Bride. Re - joice, O Bride un-

wed - ded, Bride un - wed - ded.

Second Response

Al - le - lu - i - a, al - le - lu -

i - a.

Final Hymn

When he be - held the beau - ty

of your vir - gin - i - ty and the ex - ceed - ing

splen - dor of your pur - i -

σου   ὁ Γα - βρι - ὴλ κα - τα - πλα - γείς,   ἐ -
su   o Ga - vri - il ka - ta - pla - gis,   e -

βό - α σοι, Θε - ο - τό - κε.   Ποῖ - όν σοι ἐγ -
vo - a si, The - o - to - ke.   Pi - on si eg -

κώ - μι - ον   προ - σα - γά - γω ἐ -
ko - mi - on   pro - sa - ga - go e -

πά - ξι - ον·   τί δὲ ὀ - νο - μά - σω
pa - xi - on;   ti the o - no - ma - so

σε;   ἀ - πο - ρῶ καὶ ἐ - ξί - στα - μαι·   δι -
se?   a - po - ro ke e - xi - sta - me?   thi -

ό,   ὡς προ - σε - τά - γην, βο - ῶ   σοι·
o,   os pro - se - ta - gin, vo - o   si:

Χαῖ - ρε, ἡ κε - χα - ρι -   τω - μέ -   νη.
He - re, i ke - ha - ri -   to - me -   ni.

346

ty, Ga - bri - el cried out to you, O The - o -

to - kos: What song of praise is

fit - ting for me to pre - sent to

you? By what name may I ad - dress

you? I hes - i - tate and stand in awe. But

as I was com - mand - ed I shall greet you: Re -

joice, re - joice, O wo - man full of grace.

PASCHA
Before the midnight Matins service

Δεῦ - τε λά - - βε - τε φῶς
Thev-te la - - ve - te fos

ἐκ τοῦ ἀ - νε - σπέ - - ρου φω -
ek tu a - ne - spe - - ru fo -

τὸς καὶ δο - ξά - σα - τε Χρι -
tos ke tho - xa - sa - te Hri -

στὸν τὸν ἀ - να - στάν - τα ἐκ νε - κρῶν.
ston ton a - na - stan - da ek ne - kron.

Τὴν ἀ - νά - στα - σίν σου, Χρι - στὲ Σω - τήρ,
Tin a - na - sta - sin su, Hri - ste So - tir,

ἄγ - γε - λοι υμ - νοῦ - σιν ἐν οὐ - ρα - νοῖς· καὶ ἡ - μᾶς
an - ge - li im - nu - sin en u - ra - nis; ke i - mas

τοὺς ἐ - πὶ γῆς κα - τα - ξί - ω - σον ἐν
tus e - pi gis ka - ta - xi - o - son en

κα - θα - ρᾷ καρ - δί - ᾳ σὲ δο - ξά - ζειν.
ka - tha - ra kar - thi - a se tho - xa - zin.

PASCHA
Before the midnight Matins service

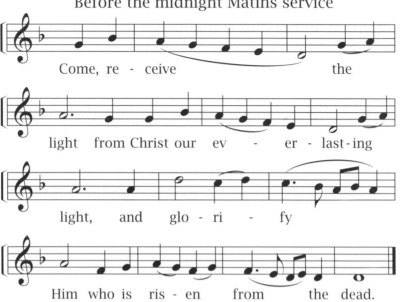

Come, re - ceive the
light from Christ our ev - er - last-ing
light, and glo - ri - fy
Him who is ris - en from the dead.

Heav-en's an - gels, Christ our Sa - vior,

sing in praise of Your res - ur - rec - tion.

Grant that we here on earth may be wor-thy al -
so to glo-ri-fy You in pur - i - ty of heart.

WEDDING

As the couple drinks from the common cup we sing
Ποτήριον/*I will take the cup,* page 324, *once only,*
without the concluding Alleluia. *Immediately,*
during the three processions, we sing the
following three troparia:

Ἠ-σα-ΐ-α   χό-ρευ-ε·   ἡ Παρ - θέ - νος
I - sa - i - a   ho - re - ve;   i Par - the - nos

ἔ - σχεν ἐν   γα - στρὶ,   καὶ   ἔ - τε-κεν Υἱ -
es - hen en   ga - stri,   ke   e - te - ken I -

ὂν   τὸν Ἐμ-μα-νου - ὴλ,   Θε - όν   τε καὶ
on   ton Em-ma-nu - il,   The - on   te ke

ἄν - θρω-πον·   Ἀ - να-το-λὴ   ὄ - νο-μα αὐ -
an - thro-pon;   A - na-to - li   o - no-ma af -

τῷ·   ὂν   με - γα - λύ - νον - τες   τὴν Παρ -
to;   on   me - ga - li - non - des,   tin Par -

θέ - νον μα - κα - ρί - ζο   -   μεν.
the - non ma - ka - ri - zo   -   men.

350

WEDDING

As the couple drinks from the common cup we sing
Ποτήριον/*I will take the cup, page 324, once only,
without the concluding* Alleluia. *Immediately,
during the three processions, we sing the
following three troparia:*

1.

O I-sa-iah, dance with joy, for the

Vir - gin has con - ceived and has

borne her son, Em-man-u - el.

He is both God and man,

and He is called the Dawn from on high.

By mag-ni - fy - ing Him, we hail the

Vir - gin as bless - ed.

351

2.

Ἅ - γι - οι   μάρ - τυ - ρες,   οἱ κα - λῶς ἀ θλή - σαν - τες
A - gi - i   mar - ti - res,   i ka - los a thli - san - des

καὶ στε - φα - νω - θέν - τες,   πρε - σβεύ - σα - τε πρὸς
ke ste - fa - no - then - des,   pre - svef - sa - te pros

Κύ - ρι - ον, ἐ - λε - η - θῆ - ναι τὰς ψυ - χὰς   ἡ - μῶν.
Ki - ri - on, e - le - i - thi - ne tas psi - has   i - mon.

3.

Δό - ξα σοι, Χρι - στὲ   ὁ Θε - ός,   ἀ - πο -
Tho - xa si, Hri - ste   o The - os,   a - po -

στό - λων καύ - χη - μα,   μαρ - τύ - ρων ἀ - γαλ -
sto - lon kaf - hi - ma,   mar - ti - ron a - gal -

λί - α - μα,   ὧν τὸ κή - ρυγ - μα Τρι -
li - a - ma,   on to ki - rig - ma Tri -

ὰς ἡ ὁ - μο - οὐ - σι - ος.
as i o - mo - u - si - os.

2. O ho-ly mar-tyrs who have fought the good fight and won your e-ter-nal crowns, en-treat the Lord to have mer-cy on our souls.

3. Glo-ry to You, O Christ our God, the pride of the a-pos-tles and the joy of the mar-tyrs, who pro-claimed to all the con-sub-stan-tial Trin-i-ty.

353

SERVICES FOR THE DEPARTED
Kontakion

Με - τὰ τῶν ἀ - γί - ων ἀ - νά - παυ -
Me - ta ton a - gi - on a - na - paf -

σον, Χρι - στέ, τὴν ψυ - χὴν τοῦ
son, Hri - ste, tin psi - hin tu
τὴν ψυ - χὴν τῆς
tin psi - hin tis
τὰς ψυ - χὰς τῶν
tas psi - has ton

δού - λου σου,
thu - lu su,
δού - λης
thu - lis
δού - λων
thu - lon

ἔν - θα οὐκ ἔ - στι πό - νος οὐ
en - tha uk e - sti po - nos u

λύ - πη οὐ στε - ναγ -
li - pi u ste - nag -

μός, ἀλ - λὰ ζω - ὴ ἀ - τε - λεύ - τη - τος.
mos, al - la zo - i a - te - lef - ti - tos.

354

SERVICES FOR THE DEPARTED
Kontakion

Μετὰ τῶν ἁγίων

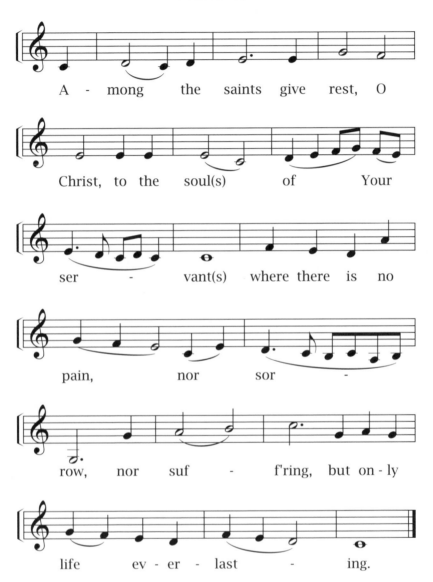

A - mong the saints give rest, O Christ, to the soul(s) of Your ser - vant(s) where there is no pain, nor sor - row, nor suf - f'ring, but on - ly life ev - er - last - ing.

SERVICES FOR THE DEPARTED
Final Hymn

in Greek

Αἰ - ω - νί - α ἡ μνή - μη. Αἰ - ω -
E - o - ni - a i mni - mi. E - o -

νί - α ἡ μνή - μη. Αἰ - ω -
ni - a i mni - mi. E - o -

νί - α αὐ - τοῦ ἡ μνή - μη.
ni - a af - tu i mni - mi.

αὐ - τῆς
af - tis

αὐ - τῶν
af - ton

or, in English

Mem - o - ry e - ter - nal.

Mem - o - ry e - ter - nal. May his
her
their

mem - o - ry be e - ter - nal.

*During the Paschal season some sing
Χριστὸς ἀνέστη/Christ is risen instead
of the above. See pages 152/153.*

356

PRAYERS

Preparation for Holy Communion . 358
Thanskgiving after Holy Communion . 360
Stewardship Prayer 362

PRAYERS OF PREPARATION
FOR HOLY COMMUNION

SAINT JOHN CHRYSOSTOM

Lord Jesus Christ, our God, absolve, remit and pardon all my transgressions, every sin I have committed by word, action or thought, willingly or unwillingly, consciously or unconsciously, forgiving me everything, since You are good and the Lover of mankind. Through the intercessions of Your most pure Mother, of the holy angelic powers, and of all the saints who have pleased You from the beginning, count me worthy to receive Your most pure Body and Your most precious Blood for the healing of my soul and body and the purification of my mind from every evil thought. For the kingdom, the power and the glory are Yours, with the Father and the Holy Spirit, now and ever and to the ages of ages. Amen.

I believe and confess, Lord, that You are truly the Christ, the Son of the living God, who came into the world to save sinners, of whom I am the first. I also believe that this is truly Your pure Body and that this is truly Your precious Blood. Therefore, I pray to You, have mercy upon me and forgive my transgressions, voluntary and involuntary, in word and deed, known and unknown. And make me worthy without condemnation to partake of Your pure mysteries for the forgiveness of sins and for life eternal. Amen.

How shall I, who am unworthy, enter into the splendor of Your saints? If I dare to enter into the bridal chamber, my clothing will accuse me, since it is not a wedding garment; and being bound up, I shall be cast out by the angels. In Your love, Lord, cleanse my soul and save me.

Loving Master, Lord Jesus Christ, my God, let not these holy Gifts be to my condemnation because of my unworthiness, but for the cleansing and sanctification of soul and body and the pledge of the future life and kingdom. It is good for me to cling to God and to place in Him the hope of my salvation.

Receive me today, O Son of God, as a partaker of Your mystical supper; for I will not betray Your mysteries to Your enemies, nor give You a kiss as did Judas, but as the thief I confess You: Remember me, O Lord in Your kingdom.

PRAYERS OF THANKSGIVING
FOLLOWING HOLY COMMUNION

Glory to You, our God, glory to You.
Glory to You, our God, glory to You.
Glory to You, our God, glory to You.

ANONYMOUS

Lord Jesus Christ, our God, let Your sacred Body be unto me for eternal life and Your precious Blood for forgiveness of sins. Let this Eucharist be unto me for joy, health and gladness. And at Your awesome Second Coming make me, a sinner, worthy to stand at the right hand of Your glory, through the intercessions of Your most pure Mother and all Your saints. Amen.

SAINT BASIL

I thank You, Christ and Master, our God, King of the ages and Creator of all things, for all the good gifts You have given me, and especially for the participation in Your pure and life-giving mysteries. Therefore I pray to You, good Lord and Lover of mankind: keep me under Your protection and under the shadow of Your wings. Grant that to my very last breath I may partake worthily of Your most pure mysteries with a clear conscience for the forgiveness of sins and for eternal life. For You are the bread of life and to You we give glory, with the Father and the Holy Spirit, now and ever and to the ages of ages. Amen.

ANONYMOUS

I thank You, Lord my God, that You have not rejected me, a sinner, but have made me worthy to partake of Your holy mysteries. I thank You that although I am unworthy, You have permitted me to receive Your pure and heavenly gifts. O loving Master, who died and rose for our sake, and granted to us these awesome and life-giving mysteries for the well-being and sanctification of our souls and bodies, let these gifts be for healing of my own soul and body, the averting of every evil, the illumination of the eyes of my heart, the peace of my spiritual powers, a faith unashamed, a love unfeigned, the fulfilling of wisdom, the observing of Your commandments, the receiving of Your divine grace, and the inheritance of Your kingdom. Preserved by them in Your holiness, may I always be mindful of Your grace, no longer living for myself but for You, our Master and Benefactor. May I pass from this life in the hope of eternal life, and attain to the everlasting rest where the voices of Your Saints who feast are unceasing, and their joy at beholding the ineffable beauty of Your countenance unending. For You, Christ our God, are the true yearning and the inexpressible joy of those who love You, and all creation praises You forever. Amen.

STEWARDSHIP PRAYER

Lord Jesus Christ, our God, accept our offerings as You have accepted the gifts of Your people throughout the ages. We offer these gifts to Your glory, for the support of the ministries of Your holy Church, for the alleviation of suffering and hunger, and for the proclamation of Your Gospel to the whole world.

Grant us Your blessing, Lord our Savior, that we may always be faithful stewards, continuing to share the gifts you have given us, by the power of Your grace, mercy and love. May Your name be glorified forever. Amen.

Index of Greek Titles

A

Ἀγαλλιᾶσθε δίκαιοι (Exalt, you just, in the Lord) 323
Ἀγγελικαὶ δυνάμεις (The angelic powers) 118/119
Ἅγιος, ἅγιος (Holy, holy) 62/63
Ἅγιος ὁ Θεός (Holy God) 38/39
Ἅγιοι μάρτυρες (O holy martyrs) 352/353
Αἰνεῖτε τὸν Κύριον (Praise the Lord from the heavens) 82/83
Αἰωνία ἡ μνήμη (Memory eternal) 356
Ἀνέβη ὁ Θεὸς (God ascends) 321
Ἀνελήφθης ἐν δόξῃ (You ascended in glory) 278/279
Ἄξιόν ἐστι (It is truly right to call you blessed) 68/69

Δ

Δεῦτε λάβετε φῶς (Come receive the light) 348/349
Δεῦτε προσκυνήσωμεν (Come let us worship) 36/37
Δόξα σοι, Χριστὲ ὁ Θεὸς (Glory to You, O Christ our God) 352/353
Δοξολογία (Great Doxology) 2/3

E

Εἴδομεν τὸ φῶς (We have seen the true light) 86/87
Εἴη τὸ ὄνομα Κυρίου (Blessed is the name of the Lord) 90/01
Εἰ καὶ ἐν τάφῳ (Into the grave You descended) 274/275
Εἷς ἅγιος (One is holy) 80/81
Εἰς μνημόσυνον (The memory of the righteous) 328
Ἐκ στόματος νηπίων (From the mouths of children) 316
Ἔλεον εἰρήνης (Mercy and peace) 60/61
Ἐν Ἰορδάνῃ (At Your baptism in the Jordan) 209/210
Ἐν πίστει τοὺς προπάτορας (By their faith You justified Your
        ancestors) 186/187
Ἐν σοὶ μῆτερ ἀκριβῶς (In you, holy mother Mary) 140/141
Ἐν τῇ γεννήσει (In giving birth) 222/223
Ἐν τῷ φωτὶ (We will walk in the light) 330
Ἐξελέξατο Κύριος (The Lord has chosen Zion) 329
Ἐξ ὕψους κατῆλθες (From on high you descended) 126/127
Ἐπαίνει, Ἰερουσαλὴμ (Exalt in the Lord, O Jerusalem) 320
Ἐπὶ σοὶ χαίρει (In you, O woman full of grace) 298/299
Ἐπεφάνη ἡ χάρις (The grace of God has appeared) 327
Ἐπεφάνης σήμερον (You have revealed Yourself) 248/249

Ἐπὶ τοῦ ὄρους μετεμορφώθης (You were transfigured) 284/285
Ἐσημειώθη εφ' ἡμᾶς (Let the light of Your face) 325
Ἐσφραγισμένου τοῦ μνήματος (While the tomb was sealed) 154/155
Ἐτοιμάζου Βηθλεέμ (Make ready, Bethlehem) 190/191
Ἐτοιμάζου Ζαβουλὼν (Make ready, Zebulon) 204/205
Εὐλογημένος ὁ ἐρχόμενος (Blessed is he) 317
Εὐλογητὸς εἶ Χριστὲ (Blessed are you, O Christ) 172/173
Εὐφραινέσθω τὰ οὐράνια (Let the heavens rejoice) 106,107

Η
Ἡ γέννησίς σου, Θεοτόκε (Your birth, O Theotokos) 176/177
Ἡ γέννησίς σου, Χριστέ (Your birth, O Christ) 198/199
Ἡ Παρθένος σήμερον τὸν προαιώνιον Λόγον (Today the Virgin goes
        forth) 240/241
Ἡ Παρθένος σήμερον τὸν ὑπερούσιον τίκτει (Today the Virgin gives
        birth) 244/245
Ἡσαΐα χόρευε (O Isaiah) 350/351

Θ
Θεὸς Κύριος (Megalynarion of Palm Sunday) 302/303

Ι
Ἰωακεὶμ καὶ Ἄννα (Your holy birth delivered Joachim and
        Anna) 228/229

Κ
Κατέλυσας τῷ Σταυρῷ (By Your cross, O Lord) 122/123
Κύριε, ἐκέκραξα (O Lord, I call upon You) 332/333

Λ
Λύτρωσιν ἀπέστειλε (The Lord has sent redemption) 326

Μ
Μεγάλα τὰ τῆς πίστεως (How great is the power of faith) 194/195
Μεγάλυνον ψυχή μου (Megalynarion of the Nativity of the
        Lord) 312/313
Μετὰ τῶν ἁγίων (Among the saints) 354/355
Μεσούσης τῆς ἑορτῆς (In the midst of this Paschal season) 166/167
Μετεμορφώθης ἐν τῷ ὄρει (When You were transfigured) 220/221
Μὴ τῆς φθορᾶς (Megalynarion of Pentecost) 310/311

364

O

Ὁ ἄγγελος ἐβόα (Megalynarion of Pascha) 304/305
Ὁ εὐσχήμων Ἰωσὴφ (The noble Joseph) 158/159
Ὁ καθαρώτατος ναὸς (Behold the temple of the Savior) 236/237
Ὁ Κύριος ἐβασίλευσεν (The Lord is king) 340
Ὁ μήτραν παρθενικὴν (For our salvation You took flesh) 250/251
Ὁ Μονογενὴς Υἱὸς (Only begotten Son) 30/31
Ὀρθοδοξίας ὁ φωστήρ (O light of Orthodoxy) 132/133
Ὅσοι εἰς Χριστὸν (As many of you as have been baptized) 292/293
Ὅταν ἔλθῃς (When You come to the earth, O God) 260/261
Ὅτε καταβὰς (When he came down and confused the
    tongues of men) 280, 281
Ὅτε κατῆλθες (When you descended into death) 102/103
Ὁ ὑψωθεὶς (Bestow your mercies) 232/233

Π

Πατέρα, Υἱόν (Father, Son) 56/57
Πλούσιοι ἐπτώχευσαν (Many who are wealthy) 342
Ποτήριον σωτηρίου (I will take the cup of salvation) 324
Προστασία τῶν Χριστιανῶν (O unfailing protection of
    Christians) 224/225

Σ

Σε τὴν φαεινήν λαμπάδα (You are the shining light) 308/309
Σὲ ὑμνοῦμεν (We praise You) 66/67
Σήμερον σωτηρία (Today salvation has come) 16/17
Σήμερον τῆς εὐδοκίας Θεοῦ (Today is the prelude of God's
    generosity) 182/183
Σήμερον τῆς σωτηρίας ἡμῶν (Today is the beginning of our
    salvation) 216/217
Συνταφέντες σοι (In our baptism) 148/149
Σῶσον ἡμᾶς, Υἱὲ Θεοῦ (Second Antiphon) 28/29
Σῶμα Χριστοῦ (Receive the body of Christ) 318
Σῶσον Κύριε (Save, O Lord) 180/181

Τ

Ταῖς μυροφόροις γυναιξὶ (The angel stood by the tomb) 162/163
Ταῖς πρεσβείαις (First Antiphon) 24/25
Ταῖς τῶν δακρύων σου (Like warm and gentle rain) 136/137
Τῇ ὑπερμάχῳ (Victorious Lady) 268/269
Τὴν ἀνάστασίν σου (Heaven's angels) 348/349

365

Τὴν ἄχραντον εἰκόνα σου (Before your most pure image) 128/129
Τὴν ἐν πρεσβείαις (She is our vigilant intercessor) 288/289
Τὴν κοινὴν ἀνάστασιν (Before Your passion) 144/145
Τὴν ὑπὲρ ἡμῶν πληρώσας (When You had joined earth to
    heaven) 278/279
Τὴν ὡραιότητα (When he beheld the beauty) 344/345
Τῆς πατρῴας δόξης σου (From my Father's glory) 256/257
Τῆς σοφίας ὁδηγέ (O You who are the source of all wisdom) 264/265
Τίς Θεὸς (Who is so great a God) 341
Τὸ πνεῦμά σου (Let Your good spirit lead me) 322
Τὸ φαιδρὸν (The joyful news) 110/111
Τὸν δεσπότην (Grant long life, Lord) 343
Τὸν εὐλογοῦντα (Lord, grant long life) 94/95
Τὸν σταυρόν σου (Before Your cross) 290/291
Τὸν συνάναρχον Λόγον (To the Word, coeternal) 114/115
Τοῦ δείπνου σου (Receive me today) 84/85
Τοῦ λίθου σφραγισθέντος (Although Your tomb was sealed) 98/99
Τῷ θρόνῳ ἐν οὐρανῷ (In heaven upon Your throne) 272/273
Τῶν ἐν ὅλῳ τῷ κόσμῳ (Throughout the world) 282/283

Υ
Ὑπερδεδοξασμένος εἶ Χριστὲ (Unending glory be Yours) 170/171

Φ
Φαρισαίου φύγωμεν (Let us flee the boastful words) 254/255
Φῶς ἱλαρόν (Radiant light) 336/337

Χ
Χαῖρε κεχαριτωμένη Θεοτόκε (Rejoice, O woman full of grace) 212/213
Χαῖρε νύμφη (Rejoice, O bride) 344/345
Χερουβικόν, Ἦχος Πλ. Β' (Cherubic Hymn, Tone 6) 294/295
Χερουβικόν, Ἦχος Πλ. Δ' (Cherubic Hymn, Tone 8) 44/45
Χριστὸς ἀνέστη (Christ is risen) 152/153

Ω
Ὡς ἀπαρχὰς τῆς φύσεως (To You, O Lord, Creator) 282/283

ISBN 0-9650957-2-X

9 780965 095723

366